WORLD'S
TOUGHEST COPS

VINNIE JONES

WORLD'S TOUGHEST COPS

ON THE FRONT LINE
OF THE WAR AGAINST CRIME

HarperCollins*Publishers*

HarperCollins*Publishers*
77–85 Fulham Palace Road,
Hammersmith, London W6 8JB

www.harpercollins.co.uk

First published by HarperCollins*Publishers* 2010

1 3 5 7 9 10 8 6 4 2

A catalogue record of this book is
available from the British Library

ISBN 978-0-00-734449-9 HB
ISBN 978-0-00-734454-3 TPB

Printed and bound in Great Britain by
Clays Ltd, St Ives plc

Mixed Sources
Product group from well-managed
forests and other controlled sources
www.fsc.org Cert no. SW-COC-1806
© 1996 Forest Stewardship Council
FSC

FSC is a non-profit international organisation established to promote the
responsible management of the world's forests. Products carrying the FSC
label are independently certified to assure consumers that they come
from forests that are managed to meet the social, economic and
ecological needs of present and future generations.

Find out more about HarperCollins and the environment at
www.harpercollins.co.uk/green

CONTENTS

INTRODUCTION

Welcome to the World's Toughest Cops. This is a no-holds-barred look at the people who risk their lives to serve and protect, in the front line of a war against drugs, gangs, gun crime, violence and smuggling. Over the following pages you're going to see just what it takes to police 10 of the world's most dangerous beats ... and meet the men and women fighting a desperate battle to keep law and order.

A couple of years ago I was asked by a TV production company to help them out with a show they were making. They were flying to meet cops in some of the most lawless places on the planet – and they were going to ride with them as they took down wanted men, busted gangs and smashed criminal organisations.

Did I fancy coming along?

Dead right I did ... I wanted to get in there for myself, on the front line. I wanted to live and breathe the danger and the adrenaline of policing some of the worst neighbourhoods the world has to offer. I wanted to make it personal.

Me and a bunch of guys flew out to see just what the score was. And we met some amazing people, had some amazing experiences. I've always believed in living every day to the full, pushing yourself to the extreme, giving whatever you do everything you have ... but these guys taught me a lesson or two about commitment. They're risking their lives, every day, because they believe in trying to protect the public, in trying to make their little part of the world a safer place.

I was in awe of them. And as for the action ... I loved it. The buzz was like nothing else I've ever known.

But there's only so much you can show in a TV programme. The cops we met were so dedicated, so extraordinary – and so much of what happened couldn't make it on to the screen, that we decided to go one further. When I was asked to write a book to take in both series – from raiding terrorist camps with the Special Ops Commando Unit in Colombia to patrolling the back alleys and no-go zones of New Orleans, from chasing cop killers in Jamaica and Papua New Guinea to busting gangsters in South Central LA – I jumped at the chance.

These are great stories; but they're also true stories. We were there.

All I'm doing in this book is showing what goes on – what these guys have to deal with day in, day out. And we weren't hiding behind minders or security men: we were right in amongst it, out with the cops in some incredibly dangerous situations, usually kitted up in bullet-proof vests. This isn't a Hollywood movie or a celebrity jaunt, this isn't us pretending to be cops for a few days … this is real. This is us embedded with 10 groups of police officers around the planet as they put their lives on the line in the name of law and order.

They are the world's toughest cops. And this is how they roll.

Vinnie Jones
LA, February 2010

ACKNOWLEDGEMENTS

This book wouldn't have been possible without so many people.

First of all I'd like to thank all the staff and crew at Zig Zag Productions who made the TV series happen, plus everyone at HarperCollins for helping turn it into a book.

Plus a special thanks to Dominic Utton.

DEDICATION

This book is for cops everywhere who risk their lives in the name of law and order … but especially for those we met, got to know and saw in action for ourselves. Proper, straight-up heroes, every one of them. It was a privilege.

HEART OF DARKNESS: SPECIAL OPS WITH JOHN OREJUELA

Colombia was always going to be a challenge. For decades, this bustling South American nation has been at war with itself: since the 1960s, government forces, left-wing insurgents and right-wing paramilitaries have all been engaged in the continent's longest-running armed conflict.

The consequences add up to nothing less than carnage. Terrorism like you wouldn't believe, guerrilla warfare, kidnapping as big business – and sometimes small – and vast, powerful drug cartels worth billions of pounds. Dense, impenetrable jungles and sprawling slums. Incredible wealth and indescribable poverty. Kids with machine-guns, rampant knife crime, casual murder, political assassinations, dead cops ... and everywhere the magical lure and deadly stink of cocaine.

Trying to control this country is a nightmare. And it means the Colombia National Police are a force like no other. To nick a line from one of my favourite films, charging a man with murder in this place is like handing out speeding tickets at the Indy 500.

Like I say, Colombia was always going to be a challenge. Not because of the violence, the danger, the risk involved in just getting in and getting out again ... but because, with so much going on, we didn't know where to start.

✯　　✯　　✯

THE YOUNG POLICEMAN stood to attention, facing a simple stone statue. In front of him, on a bed of rock, a pillar rose about 12 feet high; inscribed upon it were a few words in Spanish. Flowers had been planted around the base. Beyond lay a garden, a church, a complex of low, modern-looking buildings. Other police officers – some in uniforms, some not – passed by in silence.

Behind the lone figure, the main road to Bogotá. A Colombian flag, whipped up by the mountain wind, obscured the view briefly; but when the breeze died down again, the view to the capital was clear. High rises, skyscrapers, vast jumbled barrios and slums. Beyond that – mountains. Jungle.

The man didn't appear to notice us as we walked silently up behind him; he made no movement, not so much as a tensing of the shoulders … but we knew he knew we were here all right. He'd been trained to know – and what he couldn't be taught he'd picked up the hard way, in the field, in the firing line. Nobody was ever going to sneak up on him. This young cop was one of Colombia's elite.

We waited as he crossed himself, placed his hands behind his back in the 'at ease' position, gazed at the memorial for a moment longer, and then finally turned to greet us.

'This monument was created for all of the police officers who died on duty,' he explained. 'The last one was Wilson Reinosa, my best friend. The guerrillas planted a lot of mines in a place we had targeted. He died from a bomb there. He was married. He had a son. He was young, like 27, but a very good policeman.'

We all, involuntarily, glanced back at the memorial. When we looked at the cop again, he was smiling. 'My name is John Orejuela,' he said, extending his hand. 'I work for the Comando de Operaciones Especiales, part of the Colombia National Police. Pleased to meet you.'

The Colombian National Police Special Ops unit – or COPES for short – are a tight, elite strike force of commandos trained up for the most dangerous missions in this country. They were formed in the mid-1980s as a highly mobile, highly equipped squad for quick reaction to high-risk or crisis situations.

Only 100 of the best police officers in Colombia are good enough for COPES. Trained by the SAS and the US Marines, they operate almost exclusively in life-or-death situations. Taking on the criminal untouchables – guerrillas, terrorists, drug cartels – COPES commandos are the front-line specialists in a deadly battle to keep order.

John had been a COPES commando for nine years, and the veteran of over 100 missions. His relaxed demeanour, friendly attitude and easy-going, open features hide a seriously dedicated professionalism. He showed us his dog-tags, permanently strung around his neck, as important a piece of equipment for the commandos as any gun or bullet-proof vest.

'We don't know when we are going to die,' he explained, simply. 'So in all the operations that we do we use these – to identify us if something bad happens. Maybe a grenade, maybe a bomb.' He shrugged and grinned again. 'It's a bit dangerous … but here in Colombia, somebody has to do it. And I like the action.'

It had taken a while, but we'd found our man.

❉   ❉   ❉

Colombia is a country born out of violence. Invasion by the Spanish conquistadores in 1499 was followed by over 300 years of oppression, rebellion and tribal warfare before the country won independence from Spain in 1819 – and another seven decades before the republic of Colombia was finally declared in 1886.

And things have hardly been smooth sailing since then. For as long as there has been a Colombia, disputes between the country's two main political parties, the Liberals and the Conservatives, have had a habit of getting seriously out of hand.

In 1899 the country was torn apart by the Thousand Days War as tensions between the parties erupted into full-scale conflict – over 100,000 people died in three years – and 1948 marked the beginning of what they call La Violencia. For 10 years the Liberals, Communists and Conservatives fought in brutal, bloody clashes, mostly between hastily formed peasant militias. War crimes doesn't even begin to cover the levels of lawlessness during this time: with guns and ammo scarce, the militias used whatever weapons they could, torture and rape were commonplace, and many of the warring factions developed their own unique 'calling cards' of corpse mutilation to frighten enemies and warn traitors.

The Corte Franela or 'T-shirt cut' involves leaving dead bodies headless and with severed arms; the Corte Corbata ('Necktie cut') leaves the throat slit open and the tongue pulled out and placed over the chest; and for the Corte Florero ('Flower Vase cut'), the severed arms and legs are inserted in the torso of the victim, so the dead body looks like a crude, gruesome floral arrangement.

These horrific signatures originated during La Violencia but are still used today – by terrorist guerrillas and drug gangs for whom intimidation is as potent a weapon as death itself.

An estimated 300,000 Colombians died in the 10 years between 1948 and 1958, but even after the formation of a joint Liberal/Conservative government and the official end of La Violencia, the troubles are far from over. Left- and right-wing guerrillas continue to clash – with each other and with government forces desperate to keep some kind of control.

The official war might be over, but the killings go on.

Someone is murdered every 30 minutes in Colombia. Political assassinations are common, terrorism is rampant … but chuck in a massive kidnapping problem, crippling street-level poverty and the fact that Colombia is the world's number one producer and exporter of cocaine and you've got a crime cocktail that has left the country ravaged and reeling.

Four different units are taking on the world's deadliest criminals here. The drug squad, anti-kidnapping snipers, the Metropolitan police … and the commandos. And, of all them, it was the commandos we most wanted to see. They're the ones on call and ready to roll at a moment's notice. They're the ones able to get in and get the job done – any job – and then get out again. They're the ones with missions so secret, so dangerous, that most of them don't officially exist until after they're completed.

But we couldn't ignore the sheer scale of the challenge facing the other divisions of the Colombia National Police. Those trying to keep this country from descending into anarchy again are all putting their lives on the line in the name of a better Colombia. We couldn't gloss over the fact. And that meant getting up close and personal with officers from all four units.

Besides, we were going to have to wait for John Orejuela and COPES to get an assignment they were prepared to take us on. It would happen, they assured us.

✹　✹　✹

Before we met Orejuela, however, we had business in Bogotá.

With a population of 45 million, Colombia is one of the biggest nations in Latin America. Right in the centre of the country lies the capital, Bogotá, home to over seven million people. Here, in the poor parts of town, casual violence is a way of life, and trivial disputes are often settled with a bullet: in this tightly packed maze of narrow alleyways someone is murdered almost every day.

The cops patrolling these streets aren't about to go out unprepared. With over three million illegal firearms now in circulation, and 200 policemen killed every year, the Bogotá Metropolitan Police aren't taking any chances. They're packing, on average, two guns for every officer.

We met Sergeant Gilberto Avila, a veteran of the Met who has been deep in the barrios of Bogotá for 16 years – areas such as the poorest and most dangerous neighbourhood in the city, Ciudad Bolivar.

Avila has the look of a friendly uncle. Where the younger officers are lean, toned and wiry, and most of the other veterans are carrying seriously intimidating bulk, he's more … solid. The kind of guy you wouldn't automatically put down as tough – until you got on the wrong side of him and learnt the hard way. His jet-black hair is receding and the smile in his eyes is touched with something like sadness too. He's seen a lot of dead bodies on his beat; he's met a lot of victims.

'In this past week we've had five homicides … all from firearms,' he told us. 'The last homicide we had was two days ago. A person was killed with eight gunshots. What happened is what we call "settling of accounts".'

It's a euphemism and, like so much in this country, takes its cue from the language of big business. What it actually means, in this barrio, is another tit-for-tat killing. Revenge is a way of life here.

'He killed someone and then he was killed himself,' explained Avila. 'The family of that person looked for him to assassinate him. But we are on the trail.'

Not that those close to the victim might appreciate Avila's efforts. Sometimes, while trying to bring a murderer to justice, he can get in the way of that settling of accounts – and become a target himself. And all too often for the cops on the streets of Bogotá, it can be a case of kill or be killed. Not long before we met, Avila had recently experienced this for himself.

'They saw us coming into the area and they started to shoot at us,' he said. 'Then we fired back. Unfortunately both criminals died at the scene. It's not our intention to kill anyone. But if they shoot at us we must answer the same way.'

The few hours on night patrol we spent with Avila counted as a quiet shift – only a tense chase into the heart of the slums pursuing a local gang involved in dealing, assaults and armed robbery; and a couple of stand-offs with boys carrying knives.

One of the lads was bleeding badly. No more than 16 years old, bare-chested despite the cold night, he had wrapped his shirt around his arm in a pitiful attempt to staunch the flow of blood. The shirt was sodden, and even as we talked to him he swayed, struggling to stay on his feet. He belonged in a hospital and Avila told him so. The boy shook his head.

'What happened to you?' asked the cop.

The reply was simple. 'They stabbed me,' he said. 'I haven't been to hospital because I haven't got any money or documents.'

Avila threw his hands up in disgust, then reached into his pocket. 'But to buy this you have money, don't you?' He waved the stash of drugs he had just confiscated: basuco, cocaine residue. 'The basuco is better than medicine? He doesn't go to the doctor, he prefers to buy this.'

Avila was dead certain the kid was staying out of hospital until he had exacted his own revenge against the attackers, but there was little he could do other than take away the drugs and knife and hope the boy saw sense.

'Even when we try to help, we face the risk of confrontations,' he shrugged. 'We are the eternal enemy of the criminals.'

✵   ✵   ✵

At its most fundamental, crime in Colombia falls into two categories: street-level violence and organised terror. On the one hand there are those who Sergeant Gilberto Avila deals with every day, the poor and desperate of the barrios, fighting just to make it through another 24 hours … and on the other, something else entirely. Guerrilla groups and drug cartels operating on a level of sophistication the equal of any big business – but with a callous viciousness steeped in the Thousand Days War and La Violencia.

They would seem to be poles apart – but they share some fundamentals. Money, drugs, guns, power. And neatly wrapping up the lot is Colombia's latest growth industry: kidnapping.

In the last five years, there has been an average of over 1,600 kidnappings a year in this country. That's more than four a day and makes up around two-thirds of all the world's abductions. Thirty-five per cent of kidnaps are carried out by guerrilla and paramilitary groups for political motives – but most of the rest are purely economic.

Snatching someone and demanding money for their return has become as common a crime as mugging here, and people can be kidnapped for as little as £100 ransom.

Such an extreme problem needs a special solution.

We hooked up with Sub-lieutenant Juliet Quintero, otherwise known as Nikita. She has classic sharp South American features and clear skin that wouldn't look out of place in the pages of a fashion magazine … but make no mistake. She's deadly.

Nikita is part of the Colombian National Police anti-kidnapping unit – also known as GAULA. They are a special weapons and tactics unit, trained to carry out rescues in any environment – last year alone they secured the safe return of 136 hostages. That's one successful rescue every three days.

But Nikita doesn't exactly negotiate with the kidnappers. She shoots them.

Nikita is an elite sniper. She's usually the first on the scene and she can end a kidnap with a single bullet. But she is also the eyes of the operation, there to cover the backs of police on the ground. If GAULA make mistakes, people die. It requires a steady nerve.

Nikita, who was nicknamed after the female assassin from the movie of the same name, has been taking out criminals for four years. 'My colleagues call me Nikita because I'm a good shot,' she told us. 'So far I haven't missed.'

She uses an AR10 sniper rifle: deadly precise, it can put a hole in a coin from a full kilometre away. This means that in a rescue situation she can take up a position out of sight and range of the kidnappers and eliminate them before the ground troops storm in.

Nikita was a disconcerting person; we didn't know what to make of her. She was eerily calm when talking about her work, which was, after all, the cool, calculated shooting of men and women. There'd be no warnings before she took her shot, no 'hands up and drop your weapons' … Nikita's victims would barely even know they'd been hit – and they'd never know where the bullet had come from.

Being a sniper must always take a kind of extreme composure, an ability to detach yourself from the reality of what you're doing, but in the high-tension, high-stakes situations in which Nikita works, where trigger-happy, desperate kidnappers are prepared to kill anyone – including their hostages – in order to escape, there's the added pressure that she can't afford to make any mistakes.

We couldn't help asking her how she dealt with it. 'You start to feel the adrenaline,' she admitted. 'You have to have more control over yourself, otherwise the nerves can get into you and you can make mistakes. It's self-control.'

And she's not about to let doubts get in the way of doing her job properly. 'Even if they are criminals they are always humans,' she says. 'Of course. You don't feel any satisfaction ... but you have to take the decision to shoot or you'll let the other person shoot first.

'If I have him and I have permission, I shoot.'

It was cold – but it was also just the way things are here. And it's one thing playing a hitman in the movies, acting out a role as a pitiless, ruthless killer ... it's another thing entirely to do it for real. As your day job. If I was to get a film part playing a stone-cold assassin, I now know exactly who I'd want to talk to about what it really feels like.

Having said that, maybe her lack of pity is understandable: in Colombia, it's not just wealthy individuals who are under threat. The guerrilla conflict means the police themselves are major kidnap targets.

Barely 12 months before we met Nikita, police officer John Pinchao escaped after spending nearly nine years in captivity. He had been held by terrorist guerrillas in terrible conditions in a remote jungle encampment, his feet chained and his hands tied.

Pinchao's unit had been captured after a 12-hour siege of the town of Mitú, when up to 1000 guerrillas stormed the town, killing 16 policemen and capturing another 61. After a bloody shootout, the police ran out of ammo and were forced to surrender.

Taken deep into the Amazon, Pinchao had been given up for dead long ago – by the time of his escape, he was 33 and had spent a quarter of his life as a hostage. Most of the other prisoners had been freed in a deal with the government but nothing had been heard of Pinchao since 2003. He only managed to get away after his guards forgot to chain his feet one night during a torrential rainstorm: he fled into the jungle, surviving for 18 days on roots and animals he captured with his bare hands, before stumbling into an anti-narcotics patrol. By then he was weak, exhausted, dehydrated and starving; doctors reckoned it a miracle he was alive at all.

Nikita sees stories like Pinchao's as a warning. 'I think kidnapping is the worst thing can happen to a person,' she said emphatically. 'I won't allow myself to be kidnapped.

'When police are kidnapped it's usually in times of conflict, when they don't have any ammunition or have no cover. When I leave for an operation, I put extra ammo in my pocket. Always. Always. And if the situation arose and I had no ammo, and help could not come …' She raised her hand, her eyes locked on ours, made a pistol of her fingers and held it to the side of her head.

'If that happened I would rather take my own life than be kidnapped.'

✿　✿　✿

Nikita was hardcore, no two ways about it; and Sergeant Avila was dealing with a daily nightmare of violence and revenge on the streets … but we still didn't feel we were getting to the heart of Colombia's problems. What made the cops here different? What made them stand out among the world's toughest?

We couldn't ignore it any longer. We had to confront the worst this country had to offer. And that meant two things: the cocaine cartels and the FARC.

The FARC – which stands for The Revolutionary Armed Forces of Colombia – have terrorised the nation for over 40 years. This guerrilla force began as the military wing of the Colombian communist party, and their aim is still to overthrow the government and install a communist state. They remain the largest insurgent group in South America – and estimates of their numbers range from 10,000 to 18,000 members.

Their bloody campaign has been financed through kidnapping, extortion and drug trafficking. Tens of thousands have died in the conflict and the terrorists are responsible for more police deaths than any other form of criminal activity. It was FARC guerrillas who captured and imprisoned John Pinchao in the shootout at Mitú.

Taking them on are John Orejuela and the commandos of the Special Ops Unit. We got in touch again, asking whether we could shadow the force on their next assignment. We could, they said. But first they wanted us to meet another man. Listening to him would help us understand just what COPES are up against.

Deep in the jungles of south-eastern Colombia, 180 miles from Bogotá, lies the Colombian National Police anti-narcotics base, San José del Guaviare. Here Colonel Gustavo Chavarro leads an elite division of the drugs squad. Working closely with the Special Ops commandos, Chavarro's men are responsible for taking out the drugs at source.

Although he's got 20 years' service and 80 men under his command, Chavarro isn't afraid to get his hands dirty. 'It's a high-risk job and we in the Colombian police are aware of that,' he told us. 'But it's what we like, what we love.'

COLOMBIA

Colombia produces 70 per cent of the world's cocaine. Each year 700 hundred tons of the drug is manufactured here with a UK street value of £28 billion. If cocaine were a legitimate business, Colombia would be one of the richest countries in the world – as it is, all that wealth goes into the hands of criminals, resulting in the formation of influential, highly organised and ruthless drug cartels.

Most notorious was the Medellín cartel – headed by the worst drug lord of them all: Pablo Escobar.

Escobar ran the Medellín cartel for over a decade … murdering and bribing his way to a £2 billion fortune: in 1989, at the height of his power, *Forbes Magazine* in America declared him to be the seventh richest man in the world.

Government officials, judges and politicians were all paid off – and if they couldn't be bribed, they were ruthlessly murdered. Escobar made it a point of honour to execute anyone he considered a traitor or a threat: whether they were rival cartels, policemen, state officials, civilians, even members of his own gang – hundreds died at his word.

In the poor barrios and slums, he was known to reward street kids for killing police officers, and he once described his policy in dealing with cops as 'plata o plomo' – silver or lead. Bribes or bullets.

In 1985 he backed the storming of the Colombian Palace of Justice by left-wing guerilias: 11 of the Supreme Court Justices ended up murdered. In 1989 he was implicated in the assassination of Colombian presidential candidate Luis Carlos Galán, a liberal who had vowed to clean up the system. That same year he also ordered the bombing of an Avianca passenger plane – the aim was to assassinate just one man, another presidential candidate, but in the event another 120 people were also killed.

Five American citizens were among the dead on Avianca flight 203. For the US administration it was the last straw: Escobar had to be eliminated. In 1992 United States Delta Force operators trained and advised a special Colombian police task force, charged with locating and taking down the drug lord and wiping out his cartel once and for all.

Commandos from COPES were given US Special Forces training. They were taught that the old rules no longer applied: this was a war – and that meant that they were to do whatever it took to win.

Over 18 months the task force conducted hundreds of raids, going up against the full weight of Escobar's private army. Their tactic was simple and devastating – destroy everything that protected him, eliminate his most trusted allies. Nearly 100 of Escobar's lieutenants were killed as the commandos got ever closer to their target.

In December 1993, they finally got their man. After the drug lord was tracked down to a middle-class suburb in Medellín, the task force swooped, and in the resulting shootout Escobar was hit three times – the last, fatally, in his ear.

But if it was the end of the most powerful cartel of the 1980s, it was just the start of the modern troubles. Into the vacuum stepped other cartels … and the FARC terrorists. Between them they've carved up the cocaine trade – and taken Escobar's legacy to whole new heights of ruthlessness.

COPES can no longer manage on their own – and that's where the narcs come in.

Operating with the same military attitude – and the same level of firepower – as the commandos, Chavarro and his men are fighting the drugs trade at its most fundamental level: destroying drug crops and factories, flying deep into territory under the armed control of the cartels and anti-government guerrillas.

They've paid a heavy price: 17 officers killed and 29 wounded on recent eradication missions alone.

Chavarro told us about the last one: a raid on a suspected cocaine lab.

'It was called operation Eclipse,' he explained, 'the location, destruction and legal inspection of two laboratories that produce cocaine.'

Four Black Hawk helicopters and 46 police officers made the treacherous journey into the jungle – all prepared and expecting to face armed resistance from the drug producers. The Colombian jungle is dotted with over 100,000 hectares of coca crops, often guarded with landmines and booby traps, and they also have to be ready for ambushes. It's not something they're prepared to do without the best weapons. Chavarro's men all carry automatic machine-guns, and the Black Hawks are armed with GAU-17 mini-guns, each of which can spray the jungle with 50 rounds a second.

'God has given us the guns to defend our ideals,' he told us. 'We need good weapons. I take my men to extremely dangerous places. The only thing I want to transmit is confidence to my men – that everything will be fine. Even though I know I can't person-ally guarantee it.

'Our families know that we run high risks, and that we can die. I tell my family that the day I die in service they should be proud. But every morning when I get up I pray to God to let me grow old … I pray that he gives me the opportunity to become a grandfa-ther and see my son grow up.'

On the last raid the drugs squad were revisiting an area noto-rious for resistance to the cops – several police aircraft had been shot down here before. Ground-level commandos had identified a new cocaine lab, however, and that meant acting fast and being prepared for the worst.

Chavarro's helicopters were in the air for 40 minutes before they reached their target, a clearing in the jungle and a makeshift laboratory. After several passes of the area, every gun sweeping the dense canopy of trees that could be hiding terrorists with rocket launchers and anti-aircraft weapons, the signal was given and the choppers landed.

The squad was out and running when they had barely touched down, fanning out, fingers on triggers, ready for trouble. But as Chavarro told us with a sudden grin, this time they had been lucky. The criminals had fled at the noise of the approaching helicopters. And they'd left everything behind.

A recently harvested coca crop, chemicals and equipment for making cocaine.

A lab that size, he explained, could produce more than a ton of cocaine every month, with a UK street value of £45 million.

'So we set the explosives to destroy the lab,' he said. 'We took pictures, gathered evidence as quickly as possible – within seven minutes we were out of there again. This was an enemy area. It's an area where we were exposed to attack. We can never get too comfortable because they might attack us when we are leaving.'

Even as Chavarro's Black Hawks were rising above the jungle again, the explosives detonated, blowing to smithereens millions of pounds' worth of Colombian Marching Powder.

'It was a good mission,' he told us, but not an especially remarkable one. It's just what they do. 'It's always a successful anti-narcotics operation when none of our staff are kidnapped or injured and none of our aircraft are damaged.'

We'd heard enough. It was time to get in there ourselves. We wanted a mission. And as someone once said, for our sins they gave us one.

❖   ❖   ❖

Back in Bogotá, and our meeting with John Orejuela. As we stood at the memorial to fallen officers, we wondered just what lay ahead. Even Orejuela himself didn't know – COPES missions are so secret, so sensitive, that all details are kept classified from everyone but the highest top brass until the last minute. We followed our man into the commando HQ and he explained that the only info he had right then was that, whatever it was going to be, it was happening tonight. It was time to get suited and booted.

Inside the compound – more like a military barracks than any kind of police station – we followed Orejuela into the armoury and watched as he ran an inventory of his weapons. One by one, he methodically took the guns from the racks and checked them.

'American weapons,' he explained with a grin. 'Rifle M4.' We recognised this weapon – it's standard army issue, the kind of machine-gun they're still using in Afghanistan.

Next up was something we'd seen in films and on telly, but never in real life – and certainly never expected a cop to be handling. It was an awesome looking thing, a stubby barrel and locking mechanism maybe a foot and a half long. Orejuela checked it, then locked it expertly on to his machine-gun. Suddenly the weapon was twice the size and about 10 times as nasty. 'Grenade launcher,' he said, simply.

That just left the pistol. Standard issue Glock, with two magazines. It was strapped around his waist. 'If we have a problem with this weapon,' he indicated the grenade launcher, 'then we have this weapon,' and he hefted the M4 again. 'And if we still have a problem, then we have the pistol.' And if the pistol's lost too? Without a word he unsheathed a knife, its blade spotless, glittering, reflecting our faces even as we looked at it.

On went military-style fatigues and into a rucksack was packed headgear for night vision, and Orejuela was set. In the barracks around us, other policemen went through the same routine in silence, each concentrating on their equipment, knowing that, wherever they were going that night, and whatever they'd be up against, any slips or omissions now could mean the difference between life and death.

Finally, we followed him into the briefing room. Sixteen commandos sat at flimsy-looking formica desks, eyes intent on the commanding officer, who stood like a teacher in front of a map and an overhead projector. He talked fast, in Spanish; we couldn't keep up. Nobody asked questions, and the whole thing was over in 10 minutes.

Afterwards, we asked Orejuela what was happening.

It seemed that the police had received a tip-off about the location of known terrorists – members of the rebel guerrilla group, the FARC. Tonight, under cover of darkness, COPES were to execute a surprise helicopter raid on the remote hide-out. They were flying out at midnight precisely: the last duty of the briefing officer had been to ensure all watches were synchronised.

'We are going to look for terrorists,' he explained simply. 'It's about terrorists. We're going to catch them; there are three or four important guys they want us to bring in. We are going to have to keep our concentration because it's classified high risk, the most dangerous it can get. They will be carrying similar weapons to those we use here. They use AK47 machine-guns … The weapons that they use are very good.'

Orejuela has had many run-ins with the guerrillas during his nine years on the force.

'I'd say that on 60 per cent of operations they shoot at us. We know that the guerrillas have very good weapons. We have to be ready to fight with them.'

We hadn't forgotten where we'd met the young commando – or that he had lost his best friend on a recent operation. 'That operation was dangerous because we had 16 guys against 200,' he told us. 'And we lost five. Five policemen. It marked my life. When we lose a partner it's like losing a brother. This is my second family. It's very hard.'

But Orejuela has a reason to keep going. His father was a cop, and if that's given him a keen understanding of just how dangerous the job is, it's also instilled in him a belief that what he is doing is important. Not just for Colombia, but for his own family.

Smiling again, he produced a wallet from his pocket and fished out a photo: a boy of maybe nine or 10 years old, looking both proud and embarrassed in his Sunday-best outfit of crisp white shirt, tie and blue tank-top. He had one hand on his hip and he stared straight at the camera, his face steady, unsmiling.

'This is my son,' he said. 'I'm doing this because I want a better country for my son. Without drugs and without terrorists. Somebody has to do this job. This is my time right now.'

We looked again at the snap: the boy may not have had Orejuela's smile, but there was something in his eyes that was the same. He looked like a future cop.

If Orejuela joined the police in the first place because he wanted to follow in his father's footsteps, it didn't take long before he knew he was ready to step into the most dangerous law-enforcement job in Colombia. After just two years working the streets in the Bogotá Metropolitan Police, he put in for a transfer to COPES. He hasn't looked back.

'We do it because we love our jobs,' he told us. 'What can I say? We love it. Every week we train because we have to be ready. Everybody feels scared but we have to do it. Here in Colombia, somebody has to do it. We are prepared to do everything here – for Colombia and for our families.'

Around us, as we chatted beside Orejuela's locker, his kitbag and weapons between us, we noticed other officers stepping past, all headed in the same direction. We checked our (admittedly unsynchronised) watches – there were still some hours to go before midnight.

'They're going to the chapel,' explained Orejuela. 'For each of us this could be our last mission. Many of the men want to pray.'

※　　※　　※

Just past midnight and we were airborne. Breathing hard and crammed into a Black Hawk helicopter with 16 commandos, 32 guns and hundreds of rounds of ammunition. All the men wore their night-vision helmets – the operation was to take place under complete darkness. Everything, right down to the chopper's control panel, was blacked out.

No big-match nerves here, no psyching up and hyping up. The boys were calm. They knew what they had to do.

The target was an isolated group of houses just 30 miles from the base, where FARC members were believed to be hiding out. Intelligence had reported up to four important figures in the movement to be present, guarded by a security force of 20 men armed with AK47 assault rifles.

We were outnumbered already.

We were about to ask Orejuela about the odds, when we were silenced by a firm hand. The location had been sighted – a clearing in the jungle containing a cluster of four houses, plus outbuildings. The Black Hawk dropped fast. It was time to move in.

Dropping to a crouch from the moment they hit the deck, the commandos moved fast and low towards the buildings, spreading out as they went, each of them slipping silently through the grass, safety off, poised to react instantly and ruthlessly to any attack.

Within moments the principal property had been surrounded, every exit covered. All attention was fixed on the doors, the windows. Where would the attack come from? The door opened, spilling sudden fierce light into the blackness, and figures emerged. There were raised voices, shouting, arms in the air … but no shooting. No guns. No terrorists.

The squad leader took three men inside. What they found was not in the briefing. The house was full of people all right: men, women, children, all taking part in some birthday, christening or wedding celebration. As a thorough search of the property turned up nothing, Orejuela grew exasperated.

We'd been done. Either the intelligence was rotten in the first place … or else the FARC terrorists had received a tip-off about the approaching helicopter. Either option meant trouble of one kind or another. And Orejuela didn't like it one bit. As we wasted time in this house, the helicopter was a sitting duck, an easy target alone in the fields on the edge of the jungle – and the terrorists could easily be regrouping, preparing themselves to strike.

He beckoned us over and we sprinted towards him, mimicking the commandos' crouching run, trying to look everywhere at once, all too aware of the hidden threat in the darkness.

'It's a bit difficult because there's not just one house here,' he explained in a whisper, his eyes still scanning the surrounding trees. 'We've got three or four houses here. So when we landed in the fields they could quickly go.'

Unheard by us, the order came and Orejuela and his unit were moving again, slipping away from the first house and taking up positions around the others. If the terrorists had escaped into the jungle then there was little they could do – trying to follow them into the dense trees would be suicidal, even with their night-vision helmets. But if they had simply decamped to another building then there could still be a result to be had. Or a disaster. It was a chance they had to take.

One by one the houses were surrounded, searched, secured. It was not the ideal way of doing things and left the unit danger-ously exposed each time they moved to a new building ... but it was the only way they could work it.

Crouched where Orejuela had left us, squatting in the long grass, eyes straining in the blackness, nerves stretched to break-ing point and with every hair on the back of our necks prickling in anticipation of a sudden shout, a burst of automatic gunfire, an explosion of pain and the end of everything, it was almost more than we could handle. This didn't feel much like policing. This didn't feel like *The Bill*, *NYPD Blue*, *Miami Vice* or *The Wire*. This felt like war. This felt like ... *Apocalypse Now*.

Suddenly, like a ghost in the dark, Orejuela materialised in front of us again. He didn't seem any more relaxed. No terrorists had been found – and that was a bad thing.

'Now we have control here,' he whispered. 'We have night vision and security around the houses. Nobody can walk in here without us seeing. We have control now.' He paused and gestured with his machine-gun towards the edge of the jungle, the huge mass of trees looming at the fringes of the clearing like a tidal wave about to break. 'The problem is that the people have run. They could be anywhere. That could be a big problem for us.'

Other figures loomed out of the night: the commandos were falling back, retreating to the helicopter, preparing to leave. The guerrillas had got away. There was nothing more they could do. We returned to base empty-handed; not a shot had been fired.

With the Black Hawk whirring once again over the jungle towards Bogotá, the mood in the chopper was sombre. The operation had not been a success. But John Orejuela remained upbeat. For this cheerful, friendly, family man putting his life on the line to protect future Colombians from the worst that the terrorists, guerrillas and drug cartels could throw at them, the bottom line was that nobody died today. And that made it a good day.

'Everybody's good, everybody came back,' he said, leaning forward and flashing that wide smile again. 'No problem. What's most important is that everybody comes back.

'In this kind of operation, with the terrorists we have here, it's very difficult: they have people everywhere with radios and cell phones. And they can call: 'I hear a helicopter' and so they leave quickly. So it's difficult. But we've got to continue trying. It's difficult, it's not easy … but we have to keep trying. That's the job.'

BAND OF BROTHERS: TOE TO TOE WITH JEFF ROACH AND THE VOWS UNIT

More than any other police force in America, the New Orleans PD have had to prove themselves. After the worst hurricane in this country's history laid waste to the city, they stood alone as they struggled to keep order against a tidal wave of anarchy. They took on a flood of lawlessness … and they kept New Orleans on its feet. Just.

Their battle isn't over. The aftermath of the hurricane has left this city awash with guns and violent crime – and whole districts where teenagers with no hope of a better life take the law into their own hands.

The NOPD operate above and beyond the call of duty: and right there at the sharp end are the Special Ops unit: the Violent Offenders Warrant Squad – VOWS for short. We met some real tight outfits around the world – but none of them compared to these boys. They had faced the worst the world could throw at them – and they'd come out fighting. They were still fighting. And I was going to fight right alongside them.

New Orleans has a nickname: the Big Easy. But there was nothing easy about the job we were about to do.

❖   ❖   ❖

THE BOXING RING was in a corner of the warehouse behind police HQ. We'd noticed it before, the last time we were here, on the way to the cars … but I really hadn't planned on seeing it up this close. The canvas and ropes, the talcum powder and sawdust, the padded corners … and that smell that only boxing rings have. Sweat and disinfectant.

From outside it seemed big: I knew that once I was in there it was going to feel a whole lot smaller.

As I stretched and loosened up, the place began to fill with New Orleans's finest. They sauntered in, joking, laughing, looking forward to seeing the movie star, the former professional sportsman, the English guy, humiliated by one of their own. These were the NOPD's Violent Offenders Warrant Squad and they were all tough men, used to taking it as well as dishing it out. And I was about to go head to head with their champ. In the ring. For two rounds. For real.

I'd already been out on a couple of raids with these boys and I thought I was building up a pretty good rapport with them … but it seemed that if I wanted to ride with them on the action-packed evening shift I'd have to prove myself first. I'd heard about gang initiations, ritual beatings that new members had to endure before being accepted into the brotherhood … but I never thought I'd have to go through the same thing myself. Not with the cops.

But that's how these guys are. They're a tight, solid unit, a proper band of brothers. They won't let just anybody waltz in with a camera crew and roll with them … you've got to gain their respect first.

My reputation precedes me as a bit of a hard man – they'd seen the movies, some of them even knew about my record on the football pitch – and so they'd come up with this little initiation test for me. They wanted to see if I was all mouth and no fists … and so they asked me to face one of their own guys in the ring.

I knew they thought I'd refuse. So of course I said yes.

To these guys I'm Hollywood – but what they didn't know was that before coming out here I'd just spent six weeks in a gym training for my last movie. It may have been a few years since I'd earned a living as an athlete, but I haven't exactly let myself go. And a couple of years ago I did a film called *Strength and Honour* with Michael Madsen, in which we both played bare-knuckle fighters. I know a bit more about throwing a punch than most movie stars.

One of the guys taped up my hands and got a pair of gloves for me. I rolled my head, flexed my shoulders, jogged on the spot. I felt pretty good. I was ready to fight.

And then Jeff Roach, the unit's champion fighter, stepped through the door.

Oh shit.

He was big. Big? He was massive. He practically blocked out the light.

He strode over, stuck out a hand and introduced himself. He had about 15 years on me, at least three or four stones and a good couple of inches in height too.

We'd met Jeff before: he's the team's entry man, their top guy when it comes to smashing into properties. As one of the others had told us: 'When we find a door Jeff can't break through, that's the door I'm getting for my house.'

I asked the boys for an extra-thick headguard.

Behind us I could hear them laughing, placing bets on how long I'd last. Even our camera crew were getting involved. 'I don't know what your man can do,' we heard one of the cops say, 'but the young buck can hit hard, I know that.'

Jeff and I climbed through the ropes and squared up.

'I'm fighting for the honour of the SWAT team,' he grinned, before putting in his mouthguard.

'And I'm fighting for Britain, flying the flag for Britain,' I replied. 'So long as you don't put me on my arse we'll be fine. Cos if you do I'll kick you in the bollocks anyway.'

Jeff smiled again – and lifted up his long vest. He was wearing a protective box around the crown jewels. Everyone laughed again – seems like they really had done their research: more than Gazza ever did, anyway.

I waved away the offer of a box myself – that got me some applause, at least.

Deep breaths. Everyone was here to see me go down. Time to prove myself.

The bell rang. Seconds out. Round One.

✻   ✻   ✻

The VOWS are the New Orleans Police Department's Special Operations Unit, their elite squad. These guys are no ordinary cops; they deal with everything from tactical assaults and SWAT raids to cruising in 'wolf packs' in the city's worst areas, on the lookout for trouble.

The city is situated in the deep south of America at the mouth of the Mississippi river. It's a beautiful place with a turbulent past – some of which isn't too far in the past at all. The French quarter pays homage to its original settlers, but just a few miles away it's a different story. The after-effects of Hurricane Katrina, which devastated New Orleans in 2005, are still being felt. Violent crime in the city is amongst the worst in the United States – and it was recently ranked as having the highest overall crime rate in the country, per head of population.

NEW ORLEANS

The city is flooded with guns. Old city laws allow some New Orleaneans to carry handguns in their cars and on their person – which means that even those who aren't allowed can get them easily enough: in the US it is estimated that nearly half a million firearms are stolen every year … and an unhealthy proportion of those gun robberies happen right here.

The VOWS unit are on the front line of the crime war in New Orleans. Every day they are charged with bringing in the city's most wanted: from armed robbers and murderers to prison escapees and drug dealers. They're up against hardened criminals with a lot to lose, so a tough and uncompromising approach is always necessary.

And when they're not cruising the streets or serving warrants, they're on SWAT duty, knocking down doors and storming houses.

It's a busy job. It's also a dangerous job.

We first hooked up with the squad as they were preparing for a SWAT raid – as it turned out, we would be so impressed with them that we'd stick around to cover all the other aspects of their work too.

They had just finished their briefing when we were introduced – in the warehouse behind HQ. There was the boxing ring in the corner, but for the moment we were more interested in the fleet of vehicles parked up: specifically the SWAT truck, an armoured personnel carrier they call a Bear Cat. When one of these beasts is packed with men and charging through the streets on the way to a raid, the pumped-up, adrenaline-filled atmosphere is like the changing room at Wembley before the FA Cup Final. Times about a million.

The team came over, already kitted up in bullet-proofs and helmets, all carrying machine-guns over their shoulders and pistols round their waists. There were 40 of them, just about the whole unit, and if they were dressed for business, they were also pretty focused. There wasn't much time for small-talk and getting to know us: they were getting their heads together for the task in hand.

The target was a man wanted for suspected murder. Intelligence had come through with an address – he was holed up in a house with a girlfriend and a couple of pit bulls. But the dogs weren't the only concern: the team were also going to be looking for weapons suspected of having been used in multiple murders and armed robberies.

Trouble was expected. Shooting was a serious possibility.

According to the cops' surveillance footage, the building was surrounded by high chain fencing – as well as their guns, the unit would be taking bolt cutters. Getting into the house and on top of him before he had a chance to try anything stupid was vitally important … and that was down to the unit's number one entry man.

We spotted him immediately. He carried a kind of battering ram known affectionately as an 'enforcer' – three feet of heavy metal that he would launch at the door until it gave way – and he swung it easily by his side like it weighed nothing. His name was Jeff Roach.

Jeff's job on SWAT missions was to get the team into the property – pure and simple. Having the enforcer helped, of course … but being the size of a mountain probably played its part too. And the bottom line was that Jeff had a reputation for being the best entry man in New Orleans.

We nodded our hellos and got ready to ride.

Because of the dangers involved in the raid – and maybe because at this stage we still weren't known to the team, I still hadn't proved myself to them – we would not be allowed to sit with the boys in the Bear Cat. We watched as they loaded themselves in, psyching themselves up, adrenaline levels maxed … and then, as they pulled out, we followed behind with Lieutenant Brian Lampard in a squad car.

As we sped through the streets Brian outlined exactly what was at stake.

'The guy's suspected of murder,' he said, simply. 'He obviously has violence in his past. Depending on how bad he wants to stand his ground, it's got the potential to be a violent rush.'

Finally we came to a stop outside a detached house. Almost before we could get our bearings the truck spilled out officers and they stormed the place. The bolt cutters did their work in lightning time and then they were at the door. Jeff swung the enforcer once, twice … on the third impact the whole frame buckled and smashed and they were in, guns drawn, shouting.

The rush was amazing. We were back in the car with the lieutenant but even we couldn't sit still. We could hear screaming, yelling, dogs going crazy – and then a woman appeared, still kicking up a storm, escorted away double-quick by a couple of the men. But what was going on inside? Where was the target?

Brian's radio buzzed and he gave me the nod. There was no sign of the suspect; the house was secured; we had the green light to go in ourselves.

Even though we knew the place was crawling with VOWS boys, we still edged inside carefully, our hearts in our mouths. The place stank of dogs; dogshit was everywhere. It was a mess … but there was no bad guy.

There was, however, his gun – a weapon suspected of use in a double murder. It was still a result.

Outside again and there were mixed feelings from the team. The operation had gone well – in that no shots had been fired, no officers had been injured … and they had got the suspected murder weapon – but the target was still at large. One of the cops had a theory about that one: he pointed out a couple of kids on the corner of the street – all it takes is one sighting of a raid, one quick call, and the element of surprise is gone.

It made me angry. That these guys, who are just trying to take a man suspected of murder off the streets – and are risking their own lives to do it – should be stopped by a kid with a mobile phone. It was … disrespectful. Half an hour before, loading into the truck outside the police HQ they didn't know who would be coming home. They've got wives, families … and the fact is that on a mission like this they could have lost a man or two – just from trying to maintain a bit of law and order, just from trying to arrest a murderer. And then someone tips him off and all that adrenaline just dissolves into frustration.

It made me angry: I couldn't imagine how it must make the VOWS boys feel.

❖   ❖   ❖

It might only have been half the result they wanted, but it was still a result. The suspected murder weapon would eventually be destroyed, along with around 2,300 other firearms the NOPD recover every year. Also, I couldn't help but be impressed watching the unit in action. These boys clearly know what they're doing.

I wanted to see more. I wanted more action.

Next day the squad agreed to let me accompany a couple of officers as they served a warrant. They were going to bring in a man wanted for assault on his girlfriend and criminal damage to a property – we were going along for the ride.

But I wanted to earn my place in the patrol car and prove I wasn't just some tourist, a Hollywood actor come to gawp at the real hard men. From what I had seen of the unit they were a fiercely loyal, incredibly close team, prepared to lay everything on the line for each other: and I wanted to be a part of that.

Big Jeff and some of the others had the day off: I was to ride with Officer Fred Faff on this one. He has served on the New Orleans streets for 15 years and with the Warrant Squad for four. He was a pretty relaxed kind of guy – and was keen for me to get involved as much as I wanted.

I asked him what he thought about British policemen – he couldn't believe our Bobbies do their job without proper weaponry.

'There's no way,' he laughed. 'There's no way that I would go out on a street without a gun … Not here, absolutely not. They have criminals all over the country but in this city they are savages. They don't care about anything.'

Before long we pulled up at the target house. Made, like so many in this city, of wood, it also had a reinforced door, on which was painted some kind of weird blue hippy mural. The windows had shutters over them. Without Jeff, access was not going to be easy.

We stood and watched as Fred and the other officers knocked on the door – politely at first, and then with greater force. No answer. They rapped the windows. No answer.

We followed Fred around the side, where a locked wooden door blocked access to the back yard. 'Give us a hand here, Vinnie,' he called, and we got stuck in. Fred shimmied up the wall and tried to get some leverage from the top while I gave it a bit of gentle persuasion from the front. Finally there was a pop, a crack and a click and it swung open. We were in.

No holding me back now. 'Open up,' I shouted, hammering on windows, trying to prise open the shutters. Nobody believed the suspect wasn't in – he was simply hiding, hoping we'd go away.

Eventually, good old-fashioned determination paid off. Fred spotted him from the back of the house. 'Come round to the front!' he yelled, banging on the door. 'Come round now and let us in.'

Finally the door opened and a skinny, half-naked man appeared. His hair was all messed and he only had a pair of shorts on … but nobody could have slept through the racket we'd been making. He didn't seem too happy to see us and was now making a lot of noise himself, but the sergeant put an immediate lid on the situation.

'Get dressed,' he ordered and, with the man still protesting, raised his own voice in reply. 'Listen dude, calm it down, take it down a notch! Your girlfriend put charges on you, deal with it.'

Eventually he got into a pair of trousers and pulled a T-shirt over his head, then the cuffs went on and he was marched into the car. 'This is embarrassing,' he said, nodding at our cameras. 'You treat a man like a rat.'

The sarge just laughed at him. 'Treat you like a rat?' he said. 'How'd you treat your girlfriend? Tell you what, we'll put you in a cage and see if that's treating you like a rat, eh?'

As he was driven away, Fred and I shook on it. 'Good work,' he said. 'Getting that gate open was the thing. It opened up the whole case, right?'

He was half joking, but it still felt pretty good. The team were warming to us. What we didn't know then was they still had one initiation test planned before they were ready to let us roll with them on the night shift.

* * *

NEW ORLEANS

On the way to the bust, Fred had pointed out gaps in the houses, huge mounds of rubble and some buildings half-collapsed or with whole walls or roofs missing. The after-effects of Hurricane Katrina were everywhere. The city wore its scars for all to see.

Not all the scars were on the landscape either. The VOWS Special Ops unit were the tightest squad of men I'd seen yet – but there was a reason for that. They had a bond forged out of the worst circumstances – they'd been through things together that you and I can't even begin to imagine.

And any dangers they might encounter today pale in comparison to what they faced in 2005.

On Monday, 29 August 2005, New Orleans was hit by a storm greater than any in the history of America. Hurricane Katrina gained pace and power out in the Caribbean before unleashing a fury of biblical proportions on the Big Easy.

Katrina changed the city for ever. The storm slammed into the levees and floodwalls, ripping them apart and releasing a torrent of water. The power grid shorted, the pumping stations – so vital in holding back the sea – were drowned. Within hours, more than three-quarters of New Orleans was under water: in some neighbourhoods by as much as 15 feet.

People looked to the police – but the police were suffering too. At a stroke more than 70 per cent of the city's cops became homeless … and as well as thousands of criminal files being lost, flooding ruined hundreds of guns, bullet-resistant shields and countless rounds of ammunition.

Throughout New Orleans, citizens trapped by the rising waters and the lawlessness desperately took to their rooftops, or else barricaded themselves in where they could – often ready and willing to defend themselves with guns.

On the streets, it was Armageddon, described by one local news crew as 'a tidal wave of chaos and violence'. Stores were looted, houses were robbed, bands of outlaws and vigilantes roamed the streets, robbing, raping and pillaging at will. Police stations came under attack; paramedics were shot at; relief and aid convoys trying to get into the city were hijacked.

Three days after the storm, National Guard helicopters were brought in to evacuate critically ill patients from one hospital – they were driven off by snipers. Doctors wheeling stretchers to the helicopter had to run for their lives as bullets zipped around them.

Dead bodies floated in the dirty water, thousands more were suffering horrific injuries at the hands of the mobs ... or were simply dying from starvation, lack of water, heatstroke.

Society had completely broken down.

Into the breach stepped the NOPD. We met one of the unit who, like so many of his colleagues, stayed here to do his job. His name is Jason Samuels and if any cop we encountered around the world deserves to be called a hero, he does.

'It was almost apocalyptic,' he said, 'probably 85 per cent of the city was under water. At least three to four feet, and everywhere you had families stuck that needed rescuing. And then that other 15 per cent that was out of water, you had millions of people heading that way – basically to steal what they wanted, what they needed, just to find safety.'

Jason and the rest of the unit regrouped in a nearby school, determined to keep serving the city, putting the people of New Orleans before their own needs.

'We basically learnt the survival mentality: we went and found stores that maybe weren't flooded where we could get supplies like socks and maybe some canned food and we were able to sustain ourselves until help arrived.'

The unit spent as many hours of the day and night as they could physically manage out on the streets, patrolling the dry areas and recovering bodies from the flooded zones.

The final death toll was nearly 2,000.

But as if that whole situation wasn't enough, Jason did all this with an open gunshot wound in his leg: just over a month before Katrina hit he was involved in a shootout with a fleeing criminal while on patrol in the city. He rolled up his shorts and showed us his left thigh – long, ragged scars ran down from the groin to the knee, and a big triangle of skin like a pizza slice was red raw and tender from all the operations since.

'The gunshot wound in my groin area had never closed so I was constantly bleeding,' he said, as matter-of-fact as if he was describing a headache. 'My left leg swelled up to probably two to three times its normal size. The pain was such that I would just crawl to my boots or whatever, get dressed and go to work.'

It was unbelievable. We literally could not imagine how he did it. We couldn't really get our heads around how anyone here coped – and our admiration for the cops who put their sense of duty before their own homes and families knew no bounds ... but to do it with an open gunshot wound in your leg? To strap on your boots, haul yourself to your feet, go out and try to police the apocalypse when you could barely stand up? Unbelievable.

'As far as American police forces go, I don't think there's any other unit that has been through what we've been through,' he said. 'It was akin to going away to war together.'

We could do nothing but shake his hand. Words can't express what we thought of the guy.

No wonder this unit were so strong. No wonder they were such a team. Listening to the heroics of Jason made me proud to be serving alongside them.

And no wonder they wanted me to fight for my place on the night shift. It was time to earn my stripes. I had a date in the ring with big Jeff Roach.

✵   ✵   ✵

The bell rang and through the headguard the shouts of all the watching cops came through as a muffled roar. Word had got around and they'd turned out in force for this one. All the VOWS unit were here: and they were all looking forward to seeing their boy put the Hollywood hard man face first on the canvas.

Jeff raised his gloves in salute and moved forward. I did the same.

I was right about this ring: now I was inside, it seemed a whole lot smaller. To be fair, Jeff himself was taking up quite a bit of room himself. I was giving up a height and weight advantage – my tactic was to draw on my speed and nimble footwork to get me through this fight.

At first it worked. Jeff dominated the centre of the ring and I danced around him, popping a few jabs in. Some even got through his guard. He moved with me, watching for the most part, knocking out a couple of slow jabs himself … I parried them easily.

But then my fitness level started to tell. I may have spent a bit of time in the gym recently, but since I stopped playing football I'm nowhere near as in shape as I used to be. My legs couldn't keep up with my heart, my dancing slowed to more of a soft-shoe shuffle.

Suddenly a big right hook came out of nowhere and walloped me pure and clean on the chin. The world spun … my left knee wobbled, my right knee wobbled … I spun with it, wheeling away, managed to catch myself before I fell. Just.

The noise of the watching cops was nothing compared to the roar in my ears.

For the rest of the round I kept my distance – and most importantly I kept on my feet. The bell rang and I got a minute's rest. I made it back to the corner and sat down.

Our director – bless him, he's a lovely boy, but he's no boxing coach. He reckoned I had a shot at this. He reckoned I should play it Ali–Foreman style, use the old rope-a-dope tactic. Let him keep hitting me for another minute or two, let him tire himself out, and then slay him in the last 60 seconds, he said. Idiot.

As I took in some water and tried to clear my head I could hear a couple of the watching cops talking to the crew. 'Don't tell Vinnie now but if he beats Jeff we're going to book him. He's going to jail,' laughed one of them.

That did it for me. I came out for the second round fighting.

I'd learnt my lesson and cut out on the fancy footwork. We circled each other slower now and I kept landing my jabs. With less attention paid to dancing like a butterfly I was stinging a bit more like a bee. And, more importantly as far as my face was concerned, I was keeping my guard up. As the round went on I landed more on Jeff than he landed on me.

And that's when I saw him grinning. The bastard. Suddenly I realised – here I was, giving it my all to stay in contention, and he was cruising at 60, 70 per cent. Whenever I put a few punches together he took them … and held himself back from coming straight back at me with a big haymaker of his own.

The bell rang out and so did the applause. Jeff and I shook on it and then we both doubled up over the ropes. I've boxed for movies, but I hadn't done anything like that in a long time … and I'd forgotten that sparring for the camera is nothing like actually getting in the ring for real. You think you're fit, but after two rounds I was exhausted.

Jeff was still smiling. 'I'd have to take the first round cos I caught him with that hook, but Vinnie's got to take the second round cos he put a few punches together on me that I just couldn't defend. So we'll definitely call it a split decision.' He laughed. 'He might have thrown the fight you know, cos he doesn't want to go to jail.'

He was being generous. Let's be honest: he could have kicked the shit out of me if he wanted. He was so big and strong. Any time he wanted he could have put it on my jaw and knocked me spark out. He's the police champion, isn't he?

It didn't matter. As far as the boys from the squad were concerned I'd proved myself. I'd gone two rounds with their champ. I'd given it my best shot and despite taking a whack on the chin had kept my feet. Like the man said in *Raging Bull*: he couldn't knock me out. That's what counted.

I might not have won but I'd earned their respect. And with it came a place alongside them on the notoriously eventful night shift.

✳   ✳   ✳

When night falls, the challenge of being a cop in New Orleans becomes even greater. When the sun goes down the criminals come out to play. We'd already seen two sides of the Special Ops unit in action, on SWAT duty and serving warrants on wanted men – now it was time to run with the wolf pack.

The wolf pack is the name the squad gives to a special tactical group that hits the city's toughest neighbourhoods tackling crime as it happens, flooding an area with a gang of cars and enough men to take on the worst situations. They hunt by the light of the moon – and thanks to my battle with Jeff Roach, we'd got ourselves a place with them.

After getting stuck in helping Fred with the arrest earlier, I couldn't wait to get my hands dirty again. Officer John Barbetti was our partner tonight – he was another big guy, with the same easy confidence in his abilities as all the VOWS unit – and he assured us that if it was trouble we were looking for, there was a pretty good chance of finding it.

'There's murders here, you know, every day,' he shrugged. 'All we do is mostly proactive kind of work. Try to stop things before they happen, or while they're happening. This is the ninth ward area, so there's a lot of chasing, a lot of weapons violations, people are heavily into narcotics here …'

We peered out of the window as Barbetti drove. The streets were wide, the buildings spaced evenly out, like little Monopoly houses. It was flat, dusty, scrubby … these were the poorer areas of New Orleans and amongst the worst hit by Katrina. There were plenty of abandoned and missing houses, and most of those that remained were undergoing some kind of building work. Even four years after the hurricane, this place still needed a lot of attention.

The radio did its thing and we responded. Another unit had apprehended a suspect and called for assistance. Three or four corners later and we were on it: another of the wolf pack pulled up seconds behind us.

The suspect was standing between two officers, handcuffed, staring at his feet. Next to him a knackered old bicycle lay on the patchy grass. He was just a kid, skinny and wide-eyed. Barbetti asked what had happened and one of the guys pointed at the car.

On the bonnet: one big shiny handgun. Loaded, too. Barbetti whistled. The arresting officer filled us in, immediately lapsing into that cop-speak they use, like he was filling in a report, or giving evidence.

'I saw the subject emerge from the corner on a bicycle,' he said. 'And when he saw us he hopped off the bicycle and started fleeing on foot, digging in his pocket as he ran. So believing he was concealing a weapon, we jumped out and ordered him to stop. He continued running: as he got up into this area right here, he removed the firearm from his pocket and tossed it on to the concrete over there. So Officer Budrow tazed him and he was quickly subdued.'

Sounded simple enough. At least the kid wasn't stupid enough to try using the gun. We asked him old he was. Sixteen, came the answer. Sixteen – here he was cycling around with a loaded gun in his pocket and he's not even old enough to watch one of my films at the cinema.

It got even stranger. 'Ask him how he got the gun,' said one of the cops, a big grin on his face. 'You're gonna love this …'

We asked the kid. His excuse was about as surreal as they come. If having a good imagination was taken into consideration when judges pass sentences, he'd be walking out of court scot-free.

It seemed – according to him at least – that possessing the gun was just an accident. What he was really after was … chickens. He had been chasing a chicken underneath one of these houses when he just happened to chance across the loaded piece.

He kept the gun; the chicken got away.

Obviously we needed to get to the bottom of this. It was time for me to earn my keep and get some proper interrogation going. I wanted to see if there were any holes in his story.

'What happened with the gun?' I asked. 'Where did you find the gun?'

'Under the house,' he mumbled.

'And what was the chicken doing under the house?'

'I was chasing the chicken.'

'Why were you chasing a chicken?'

'To sell it for clothes and stuff,' he said, like it was the most obvious thing in the world. 'You can get 10 dollars a chicken.'

Ten bucks? How come they don't cost more when I get them from the supermarket? I moved on.

'Are you quick enough to catch a chicken?' I asked. We've all seen *Rocky*, we all know that scene where he tries to catch the chicken. If Rocky Balboa couldn't do it, I was struggling to see how this skinny kid could.

'Yeah,' he shrugged.

'You sure? How many do you get in a day?'

'I didn't get none: I found the gun, I was going to sell it.'

It was his story and he was sticking to it; but it had also got him tazered for his trouble – 50,000 volts of electricity disabling his nervous system, knocking him out more effectively than a big right hook from Jeff Roach. We asked him how it felt.

He raised those big, wide eyes and looked at us properly for the first time. 'I was shaking like a chicken,' he said.

We couldn't help but laugh ... even though we knew that it was really no laughing matter. In New Orleans even 16-year-olds are involved in serious crime – young though he was, to the cops here there simply wasn't anything that unusual about a kid of his age carrying a loaded gun in his pocket.

'A lot of the armed robberies and now even the murders, the suspects are getting younger and younger,' explained one of them. 'So who knows what he had on his mind, you know?'

* * *

The point was made even clearer to us as the night wore on. The wolf pack drove through the ninth ward on a steady mop-up operation, racing from one incident to the next, pulling over suspicious-looking people on stop-and-searches, flagging down cars they didn't like the look of … and responding to reports of shootings, muggings, drug-dealing.

And all too often, the people we were questioning, handcuffing, taking away to the cells, were younger than my own son. Officer Dave du Plentier, NOPD veteran of 18 years' standing, explained that that was just how it was these days. 'Look at all these people right now, in these cars and in handcuffs,' he said, as we joined him after yet another take-down. 'Look at their faces. They're kids, they're children and you look at the hardware that they're carrying out here. The rifles, the guns.'

According to some reports, as many as 50 per cent of teenagers drop out of high school across this state – and, in the poor areas of New Orleans especially, many of them turn to crime to make a dollar.

'By the time we get to see them, the only thing you can tell them is death or jail,' said Dave, 'and guess what? They don't care about either one. Jail is almost like graduating from college for kids out here, it's like a pen on their shirt. They just do their time, learn in jail and come back out and keep doing it.'

On just the one night shift with the wolf pack we must have seen nearly a dozen suspects questioned, cautioned, chased or arrested – most of them, it has to be said, were teenagers. I did my bit too, talking to them, checking stories, filling in back-up units and helping look for anything dodgy that might have fallen out of their pockets … and the more work we did, the more I got into it.

It was high-adrenaline, edgy stuff: and it was about to get a whole lot more edgy. I was beginning to think like a cop a bit too much for my own good.

※　　※　　※

Back with Barbetti and we'd received a call to respond to yet another stop-and-search when the unit ahead spotted a suspicious car at the junction. Almost before we could radio them back, the car took off, tyres squealing as it disappeared down the road in a cloud of dust.

Barbetti floored it and we sped after them. Houses zipped by in a blur as the speedo clocked up 50, 60, 70 ... when we hit 80 they were still outrunning us. More gas – and at 100 miles per hour the dust thrown up by the car ahead meant that visibility was down to practically nothing.

Barbetti spoke low and fast into the radio, his voice barely audible over the scream of the siren – and suddenly we were braking, turning, swinging a hard right and then a vicious left before gunning full ahead again. We were on a road parallel to the target now, Barbetti pushing his car as hard as he could to try to cut him off. We flew over one intersection, then another, before the radio burst into life again.

'We got a runner!' he said, slamming the brakes and turning left again. The other chasing unit had reported that the suspects had crashed and taken off on foot. We skidded to a stop and jumped out. 'He's right around here someplace,' he said, one hand on his holster, the other swinging a torch. 'Keep an eye out behind us.'

There were more vacant lots here than occupied houses – some plots didn't have any buildings on them at all and nature was reclaiming the ground. Sick-looking, stunted bushes, long grass, even trees were growing just off the road – meaning we couldn't get a clear line of sight for more than a couple of metres. There were plenty of places to hide here, and so far there was only us two units on the scene.

Suddenly I spotted a man legging it across the road and into the bushes. Barbetti saw him at the same time and took off. 'Come here! Get down, get down, get down!' he yelled, and dived into the darkness after him.

We looked around. Where was back-up? Barbetti had gone after the runner and suddenly we were totally alone. More to the point – what if the big cop wasn't fast enough? Somebody needed to head round the other side, cut him off, catch him coming out.

There was nothing for it. Pulling my bullet-proof vest tight, I took a deep breath and sprinted hard over the road, skirting the scrub on my right. Call it brave, call it foolish, call it what you like – the adrenaline had kicked in and after all my experiences with these boys I wanted to grab the chance to show what I could do.

I honestly didn't think about my own safety, not right then. We'd just come off the back of a 100-mile-an-hour chase after a night of taking down kids with guns and I had the wind up me. If I could nail this guy I was bloody well going to.

I cut diagonally into the vacant lots and burst through the bushes, every nerve straining, every muscle ready to floor the bastard ... and nearly ran straight into the cops from the other unit. They had him on the ground, were slapping the cuffs on, and when they saw me come thundering through one of them held up a hand. 'We got him, Vin,' he said.

Just then Barbetti came charging out of the trees on the other side. Call it a pincer movement then – I may not have notched up my first take-down, but we couldn't have co-ordinated it better if we'd planned it. Like flushing out a rat.

One down. But there was still another at large.

The boy we'd chased down – and, like all the others, he was just a boy, another teenage kid who'd fallen through the cracks in the system – confirmed that he wasn't alone. The car was stolen, he said: but it was the other guy who stole it, when he got picked up he didn't even know it was nicked. He said he didn't know if his friend had a gun.

The Canine Unit was called. In this jumble of empty and smashed-up houses, derelict plots and scrubby wasteland, there were a million places to hide. Dogs might just give us the edge.

As they did their work, we moved with them. All the cops searched with guns drawn and we shadowed them, scouring the area ourselves, eyes peeled, senses straining for any sign. I still hadn't come down from the rush of chasing the first suspect: right then I wasn't thinking about my family, or my career, or even making a TV show about these guys – all I was thinking was how we needed to find this kid. If I could help, I would help any way I could.

And for their part, the squad were right there with me. Nobody questioned what I was doing, nobody asked me to hang back and leave it to the professionals. Finally, it seemed, I was one of the team.

We searched for over an hour. We went through every garden, every abandoned house … the dogs snuffled and sniffed, and we followed them, peering and probing every nook and cranny of the neighbourhood. We couldn't find him. He'd disappeared, like a ghost into the New Orleans night.

Back at the car, Barbetti wasn't too downbeat. 'Listen, man,' he said, 'you did a good job tonight. You did a good job spotting the guy. It was good eyesight and it led to an apprehension. And as for the chase … that was something else. There's one more criminal off the street right now.'

The chase. The adrenaline was wearing off and the reality of what I'd done was beginning to kick in. We'd seen so many guns in this city … thank God there were none involved right here. We left with hearts still hammering.

✳   ✳   ✳

The New Orleans VOWS unit were unlike any other squad we encountered. If gaining their trust was difficult – and I still had the bruises to show it – then once we'd been accepted, it was magic. Rolling with them, becoming part of the team, getting involved … it was amazing how much I got into it. It felt like I was one of them.

It was only later that I fully appreciated the danger I'd been in. Before we quit the Big Easy, we hooked up with Jeff Roach again – he'd heard about our chase and he told us a story that seemed to sum it all up.

'There was one time,' he said, 'we were looking for a guy wanted for second-degree murder … he was tall, like six-three, but he was slim – and we couldn't find him anywhere in the house. So I go in the bathroom, and I don't know how the houses are done in the UK but there was a laundry chute, where you put the laundry in and it just drops to the ground, right? And it's like, a couple of feet wide at most, and I had holstered my gun and I was just looking at things, cabinets and whatnot, and I flicked that cabinet open and the guy was in there.'

He laughed. 'I mean, his knees were by his face and literally you couldn't have fit another inch in there, so I jumped back and I drew my gun, said 'Lemme see your hands!' and he could barely show me his hands, so we pulled him out and we got him cuffed. And after he's out we see there was a wig in there, right?

'And the sergeant said to me, "Lucky he didn't have a gun!" …
I moved the wig and there's a 9mm pistol right there. If he could
have moved his hand he'd have had me. I laughed then but I got
home and I was like phew … I really looked in the mirror on that
one, know what I mean?'

We got it loud and clear. I was lucky, I said. We shouldn't have
taken the risk.

He grinned again. 'One thing cops here say: sometimes we're
lucky – sometimes we're good. One of our captains who was in
command during Katrina: he always used to say, "It's better to be
lucky than good – but when your luck runs out you better be
good."'

'You got the guy. You did good.'

RAGING BULL: ON THE FRONT LINE WITH ANDRE STEYN

Durban lies on the east coast of South Africa. The busiest port in the continent, it has a population of nearly three and a half million people, and its sandy beaches and subtropical climate have made it a popular tourist destination.

But like everywhere in what they're calling the 'Rainbow Nation', a new society of equality and optimism, Durban has its problems with crime.

There's not a whole lot of optimism on the streets. And there's not too much equality either. From armed robbery and gun violence to ATM bombings and carjackings ... those getting left behind by the vibrant new South Africa are taking the law into their own hands.

Battling against the crime epidemic is the thin blue line of the South African Police Service – a line stretched almost to breaking point. They're the ones desperately trying to maintain order against all the odds here; they're the ones trying to prop up South Africa's wholesome new image as a safe, friendly place in which to live, work and to holiday. And, right there at the sharp end, often first on the scene, is the Flying Squad, a mobile unit that deals with anything and everything that Durban's criminals have to offer.

We were embedded with Andre Steyn, an inspector with the Flying Squad – a man who knows these streets better than anyone out here ... and who takes his life in his hands every time he clocks on for another shift.

Back in my playing days I once said there weren't many footballers I'd want beside me in the trenches. Well, I'd want Andre Steyn.

✺   ✺   ✺

THE MAN IN THE ORANGE TOP and baseball cap shielded his face, turning away and hunching his shoulders. He spoke in a low voice – so low that the cops surrounding him had to lean in to catch his words. We couldn't pick up anything he was saying.

The officers' voices came through loud and clear, though. They hit him with a barrage of questions – and leading the interrogation was Inspector Andre Steyn.

'How are we going to get into the vehicles?' he demanded. 'Are they locked? We don't have a warrant to break the window. If you're a hundred per cent sure ...'

Another cop joined in. 'Where were the guns fired? Was it outside the club? If we go into the club we are not going to get out the back.'

Steyn again: 'What are the suspects? Coloured males? White males?'

We were in an underground car park in the centre of Durban – and something big was about to go down. It was past 10 p.m. but Steyn and his team from the Flying Squad were just getting into their stride: their informant had word that security men at a popular nightclub were carrying illegal guns. As they hit their source for details, the air crackled with restrained adrenaline, each of the officers itchy to get going, but smart enough to know that doing so unprepared would be suicide.

'Will they give over the firearms or will they fight? What is the score?' demanded Steyn.

Finally, we picked up an audible answer. It wasn't exactly the one we were hoping for. 'They're not just going to give you them like that,' he muttered. 'You can expect something. They can give you a fight.'

One of the squad chipped in. 'Right,' he said. 'We hit the outside, then after that one of us has to go inside. Into the offices. Not into the club itself. We can maybe take him into the office, check the office, the safe and all things like that.'

There was a moment of silence, as each of the men took in the info and prepared himself for what was to follow. In the car park the strip lighting hummed and flickered, casting a weird glow over the faces of the cops, before the silence was finally broken by the man we were here to shadow.

Steyn turned to us and grinned. 'Are you coming? This may be peaceful, maybe not peaceful. It depends on how quick we hit them and how surprised they are. They want to fight? They get fucked up, bro.'

Were we coming? Are you joking? It had been a hell of a night so far … and it was just about to get a whole lot more intense.

❈   ❈   ❈

Andre Steyn has been an officer with the South African police for nearly 20 years. He's built like a bull – squat and powerful, with a shaved head like a bullet and the forearms of a wrestler, and he's made even more bulky and imposing by the body armour he wears the whole time we're with him. During the day his eyes are hidden behind wraparound shades – at night, you can see they're steely blue, unwavering, steady. And he's under no illusions as to the dangers of his job.

'In the Flying Squad you can get any incident,' he told us. 'Police-men get shot, hijackings, armed robberies, house robberies, shooting incidents … you name it, day to day. When a policeman goes to work you never know what to expect. You never know what's over the hill. Can be armed robbery, can be a house break-in, you can get shot down. When you say goodbye to your loved ones at night, you never know if it's the last time.

'Because so many policemen get killed in South Africa, you live day by day. You just have to enjoy the job you do.'

He wasn't exaggerating, either.

South Africa may be known now as the Rainbow Nation, a country freshly emerged from its troubled and bloody history – but it still bears the scars of its past. For 43 years it was a state divided by the rules of apartheid: where the black population were stripped of their citizenship and denied their basic human rights.

With it came oppression and violence. As civil rights leaders like Nelson Mandela and Stephen Biko were imprisoned or murdered, the population divided along ethnic and economic lines. Massive townships sprang up on the edge of the cities, becoming homes to millions of blacks and Indians who'd been forced out of 'whites only' areas. Without investment, facilities and often even basics like running water, they were in stark contrast to the luxurious homes of the white minority rulers.

Resistance grew, however … until, finally, Nelson Mandela's long walk to freedom in 1991 saw him released from jail and apartheid was abolished. Black and white, rich and poor: everyone was equal now. The shattered country could set about rebuilding itself.

That was the idea, anyway. But if all men were now equal in the eyes of the law, the chasms which divided society for so long have proved less easy to repair. This is still a country of terrible economic inequality, and with the old barriers torn down, crime has rocketed.

The end of apartheid was a new dawn for South Africa, but with it came a terrible hangover and a whole new reputation to live down. A new horror fills the lives of citizens – black and white alike: gun violence.

Each day, more than 300 murders and violent attacks take place here; this country holds the dubious distinction of being the number one nation in the world for assaults, rapes and murders with firearms. In South Africa, there are 50 murders a day and every three days a cop is killed.

South Africa has a population of around 47 million people – that's six million less than the combined total of England and Wales. Yet in the same year that those two countries witnessed 757 murders, South Africa saw 18,487.

Every year in this place over 100 police officers are killed in the line of duty – roughly two every week. In the UK there have been less than 100 officers killed in the last 50 years.

It's what makes being a cop here one of the most dangerous jobs in the world. And for Andre Steyn, it's especially so. As an officer in the Flying Squad, he's part of a rapid-response unit dealing with the worst the country has to offer – often acting on instinct, relying on a heady cocktail of training and adrenaline to get him through each shift.

'For every policeman it's a dangerous job, but ours is just different because we respond to situations as they happen,' he explained. 'Any emergency that comes through, we respond. So we're the first vehicles standing off. You have to be ready for everything; you never know what can happen. It can spark and then you have to be ready for it.'

We were rolling with Steyn on an ordinary night in the streets of South Africa's third city. This was to climax, it seemed, with the takedown of doormen wielding machine-guns outside a city-centre nightclub, but the hours before weren't exactly short of incident either. And Steyn himself, we would find out, was no ordinary cop.

❈   ❈   ❈

The speed at which South Africa has transformed itself is staggering. From global outcasts, the West's dirty little secret ... to shiny, progressive tourist hotspot and World Cup hosts: and all in less than 20 years. It's change at a breathtaking pace, a roller-coaster ride of reform and renovation.

Some might say it's happening too fast. Some parts of society just can't keep up.

And that speed, that urgency, seems to seep through everything here. To outsiders, visitors like us, the effect can be dizzying. Our night with Andre Steyn fitted the same pattern: it was breathless, non-stop, a race against time. There wasn't a moment to take stock, there wasn't a second to spare. We sped from one incident to another, covering everything from drink-drivers to dead bodies – and all at a tension level we didn't experience anywhere else.

Sure, we had scary moments in every place we visited: but in Durban, speeding through the streets with the Flying Squad, chasing the worst this place had to offer, we couldn't relax for a moment. There just wasn't time to think.

Andre Steyn isn't afraid, however.

'It was my passion to become a policeman,' he told us. 'I grew up in a military family, I shot my first gun when I was five or six years old. That's how I grew up. It's in me.'

Steyn spent some time in the army in 1991 – the year after Nelson Mandela was freed – and in 1993 enrolled at the Police Academy in Chatsworth, a township originally created for the Indian population of Durban. 'I was in the first white intake there – and it was like a holiday camp because we were fit from the army,' he laughs. 'But, yeah, they teach you the basic police work there: armed SWAT, armed driving, tactical training, computer stuff – you name it, you do it.

'When I finally became a cop on the streets I was very excited,' he continued. 'Yeah, bro – you get your badge, you can't wait to get your gun, your pistol … I just wanted to get to the job, you know? Work, work, work.'

Work, work, work. Our night with Andre Steyn was work, all right. Hard work, fast work, dangerous work. And, at least it seemed to us, work without a strategy. Maybe that was going on back at HQ, in the corridors of power – but if so, we didn't see it. Where we were there just wasn't time. Steyn and his partner were too busy out on the streets, dealing with it all.

✵   ✵   ✵

Steyn had got word of the meeting in the car park whilst on patrol. The informant had come forward that evening; the Flying Squad would strike that night. It's the way things work here.

When the call came through we had already been out with Steyn and his partner John Chapman for hours – and we'd seen enough action to fill a whole series of programmes.

Steyn's a pretty daunting-looking guy at the best of times: it just so happened that that particular night he was especially fired up. We watched him sign out, load up and double-check his weapons in silence, then followed as he led us into the patrol car. The last of the evening sun had turned all of Durban gold, sparkling off the high-rises and shopping centres, and as we slid smoothly along the highways it was easy to forget that we were in one of the most dangerous cities in the world.

He was about to remind us just how dangerous. The night before, an ex-girlfriend of his had been the victim of a carjacking.

Carjacking is one of Durban's most common crimes – and one of its nastiest. Victims are jumped getting in or out of their vehicles, sometimes even when they're simply waiting at traffic lights, and forced to drive to one of the townships at gunpoint. Once there, the lucky ones will be robbed and left to find their own way home. All too often, however, the victims are raped, assaulted, even murdered. Most carjackers in Durban are armed with cheap, illegal weapons, including pistols, 9mm semi-automatic machineguns, even AK47s.

In the Kwazulu Natal district, of which Durban is the capital, carjacking has grown by 40 per cent, and now more than 70 cars are hijacked every single week.

With his eyes unreadable behind the wraparound shades, Steyn filled us in with the details.

'What happened was that my ex-girlfriend got hijacked last night,' he said, his voice clipped, short. 'She went to pick up her son from a fitness class at the gym and a blue Corolla followed her in. Two guys wearing overalls grabbed her – she thought it was her son joking around – but they put a gun to her head, told her to jump in the back seat and they sped off with her in the car. They were driving around with her for 10 minutes before they said, look we don't want to rape you or kill you, we just want the car and jewellery and anything else you've got.

'They dropped her in Effingham, which is the north side of Durban, on the side of the road, and they gave her her phone back so she could go phone someone. Eventually a guard vehicle picked her up.'

He paused, stared out of the window at the city flashing past, one hand toying with the holster of his sidearm.

'When I got the call that she had been hijacked and they took her with them in the vehicle, I thought, she's a beautiful girl, long blonde hair, she's going to get raped, shot in the head or something. And she's got a son, a good rugby player, so I really thought, hey, what must I do now? If she gets shot I've got to try and find the body, you know? Not a good feeling. Thank God nothing happened.'

We asked him how he felt about it now, starting another shift.

'It feels weird,' he said. 'I was very angry last night, because I'd just finished shift and you work the whole day thinking about the theft of motor vehicles, hijacking and so on, and then you just come off duty and it happens to someone you know. You get a lot of anger, yeah?

'There was nothing she could do. She was a harmless woman – why go for a harmless female? Cowards, that's what they are.'

He paused again, and flashed that quick grin. 'But as I say, every dog has his day. If they must keep on hijacking, if they must keep on doing what they want, then one day they might drive into my police car … and then they are over. Know what I mean?'

As if on cue, his partner Chapman pointed silently out of the window and Steyn snapped back into cop mode. A car in front was behaving suspiciously – we watched as it jumped first one, then another red light.

As we accelerated towards the vehicle, Steyn was already reading the licence plate number into his radio – though as he pointed out later, the problem with carjackings is that the victim doesn't have time to report the car as stolen, or at least not until it's too late.

Within seconds we were hard on their bumper and Chapman gave them a flick of the siren. 'Pull your vehicle off!' ordered Steyn through a loudspeaker, 'Pull off now!' As the car slowed and parked, we were right behind them.

The sun had set now, and outside there was no light other than our headlights. The occupants of the car were just silhouettes: we could see they were two men, but little more than that.

Ordering us to stay put, Steyn and Chapman drew their weapons and cautiously approached. As they stalked towards the car, half-crouching, side-on, flanking the vehicle, hands steady over their guns, Steyn barked orders. 'Switch your car off. Get out. Get out. Let me see your hands. Get out of the car NOW.'

The two men emerged, slowly, arms raised. To be fair, they looked terrified. 'Turn around,' they were ordered. 'Hands on the roof.' Both were patted down quickly, expertly, and everyone relaxed a little.

But not much. 'Why did you run two red lights?' demanded Steyn, his weapon still drawn. 'Where's your driver's licence? How much have you had to drink?'

These boys weren't carjackers – but the driver was under the influence. This time they were let off with a slapped wrist … But none of us had ever seen a drink-driver questioned at the point of a machine-gun before.

'A lot of policemen get shot in South Africa when they just walk up to the car,' explained Steyn. 'You can't just walk up to the car and just say, "Hello sir, get out of the vehicle." It's totally different here. They can fire at you. They can shoot you stone dead. Before you know it, your partner's on the ground and you can't react. So you have to approach every car tactically. That's how you survive.'

He wasn't just reciting training manual theory, either. Steyn and Chapman recently chased and confronted a car containing four armed robbers. It was a chase that quickly became lethal.

'As we approached the car the guy started firing,' he explained. 'The bullets hit the wall behind us, shrapnel hit our bullet-proofs. Came past us like that … unfortunately I had to shoot back at him.'

We pulled back into the Durban night-time traffic and Steyn didn't seem about to offer any more. So ... we eventually asked him what happened. 'Oh, he was deceased,' he shrugged. 'The other three ran away but the next day they were found in hospital with bullet wounds.'

'So you took one of the guys down,' we interrupted. 'How did that feel?'

'How did it feel? I don't know, I had to take him down because he shot at us. It feels the same way as how they feel to take us down. They're happy about it. If he wants to shoot at the police he can be our guest. If we shoot back and kill him, it's sad but what can you do?'

If there was any regret, remorse or turmoil in Steyn's mind about killing a fellow human being, it certainly didn't show. That's just how it goes for these guys. In the big cop's own words, that's how you survive.

* * *

We were about to find out for ourselves just how flimsy the line between life and death really is. We'd hardly been back in the car a few minutes when the radio crackled again and we were once more flying through the streets. This time there had been a confirmed carjacking – and it had ended messily.

At the scene itself, cop cars and ambulances lay strewn all over the street like toys thrown down by a toddler. Every siren was flashing, every headlight was on full beam. The streets buzzed with noise: civilians chattering or giving statements; policemen questioning bystanders, looking for witnesses, radioing amongst themselves; medics snapping out quick, precise instructions.

Most of the crowd was gathered around two ambulances in particular. Following Steyn to the centre of the action, we were just in time to see a body bag zipped shut. In the other wagon we made out a pair of bare feet on the stretcher as a couple of paramedics worked furiously around the body. But those feet weren't moving much; they didn't look too good at all.

'Watch your step,' someone warned. Right in front of us, splattered across the street like someone had smashed open a big tub of red paint, was a massive amount of blood. Puddles of it. How much blood is in the human body? Ten pints? It looked like more than ten pints here.

Steyn sauntered around the scene, exchanging words with officers and witnesses, asking short questions, listening to long answers. It seemed that this was the scene of a carjacking gone wrong. Someone had attempted to steal a car – but had ended up getting chased by another three vehicles. They managed to force him off the road, but after he crashed, he came out shooting. Two people caught his bullets: one of them died instantly, the other was still touch-and-go. And the shooter? He was still at large.

'As soon as he collided on the wall, he got out and started shooting, shooting everyone that was on the street,' we were told by a woman who had seen it all happen.

Steyn shook his head and we left. There was nothing he could do here. The regular cops were already all over this one.

Carjackings make Steyn angry. Because of his ex-girlfriend the night before … but also because even this rhino of a man had himself been a victim.

'It was three of us going on fishing trip down the north coast,' he told us. 'We left at midnight and at about three o'clock a vehicle came down behind us with about five or six men and they started flicking their lights at us, so we pulled over. And as we did they shot at us. I had my firearm, I pulled back, I shot back at them. I only had two magazines, they came from the front and from behind us at the same time, shooting at us with AKs.

'They pulled a hand break turn right in front of us, and we all jumped out and ran into the bushes. They all came around the vehicle as I was lying in the bushes, it was dark, I had no ammunition left, and they took the car.

'I went for help, I came out the bush, into a place where I finally found a phone, and phoned the police, and they came and picked us up. Eventually a week later they got arrested. One of them had got shot dead – so I got one of them out of six.

'They had two AKs, a shotgun and a nine millimetre. The main guy got 30 years, and two of the others 15 years each. The rest walked free due to lack of evidence.'

We couldn't help wondering what would happen if Steyn ran into them again.

'I will do what's right,' he said, with an emphatic nod of his head. 'They fire on me I will take them down, it's the only way I can do it. To save me or save my partner's life you have to fire at them. I've been in a lot of gunfights and you have to fight fire with fire. But to answer your question, if I came across them again they will be lucky to survive, very lucky.'

One dead out of the six men who fired at the policeman. It wasn't enough for him.

We pulled back into the street, easing away from the murder scene with a quick blip of the siren by way of a farewell, on to whatever came next.

*　　*　　*

The pattern of the evening was set. There was to be no order, no storyline to our shift – just a succession of high-octane, danger-filled incidents, stacked up almost quicker than we could handle them, leaving no time to think in between.

Not all crime in this country involves violence against persons. Cash machines are a target for criminals in South Africa, just as they are in Europe and America. But subtle methods of cloning cards, skimming, stealing data and filming PIN number entry have been rejected here in favour of a less sophisticated approach.

They simply blow the thing up.

When I played for Wimbledon we used to be accused of something they called Route One football – where the ball was lumped towards the goal as quickly as possible, with no time for finessing or fannying around. Well, call this Route One robbery.

The usual pattern is for a group of four or five heavily armed men to approach a secluded ATM in the early hours of the morning. They plant dynamite sticks around it and simply hope they hit the right spot. Each terminal can hold up to £10,000, twice the average annual wage – which makes them a seriously tempting alternative to a nine-to-five. And as a result, ATM bombings have become one of South Africa's most fashionable crimes. There were 54 incidents in 2006: the following year the figure had risen to 387.

'Cash in transit' robberies are also on the increase. Just as unsubtle but with an added ruthless disregard for human life, they involve a gang ambushing a security truck, holding it up at gunpoint and making off with the money. In the last seven years incidents like these have more than doubled, and more often than not they result in the death of security guards and innocent bystanders.

'You know why it is?' asked Steyn. 'It's because of the movies. That movie *Heat*, where they ram the truck. That movie came out and suddenly it started … cash in transits started. That's how they do it. They see something at the movies and then try it.'

More conventional house and business robberies are also up – in South Africa as a whole by 50 per cent in a single year. And Durban is the robbery capital of the country, with more than three thousand taking place here every year.

Our next call was to the scene of one such crime.

Once again, it started with a radio alert – and once again, the short conversation was barely finished before the accelerator was floored and we were eating up the miles. But this time it was sirens off. A robbery in progress had been reported and if the bad guys were still there we didn't want to go scaring them away.

The neighbourhood we cruised into was by far the most respectable we'd seen yet – detached houses set back from the road, with high walls and gates to keep intruders out. Not that they seemed to have done much good tonight. Chapman pointed out the building in question and we eased up outside, moments before a police van that had been following us also slid to a halt.

We watched from the car as Steyn and his partner, guns once again unholstered, crept through the garden, eyes swivelling. The front door stood wide open, spilling light. Steyn motioned to the four men from the van to move around to cover the rear exit. He gave them a minute to get into position and then, moving with surprising speed for a man his size, ducked inside. In one hand was his semi-automatic, in the other his torch, held in typical cop style, enabling it to double up as a truncheon if necessary.

There was no noise from inside. We were holding our breath, waiting for the shouts, the gunshots, the screams … After what seemed like an age but was probably barely a minute, Steyn reappeared in the doorway and motioned with a jerk of his shaved head for us to follow.

Inside was chaos. What was once a well-kept family home now looked like the aftermath of a riot. Furniture was tipped over, smashed, everything at crazy angles, the floor littered with debris. Drawers had been pulled out, a mirror smashed. We followed Steyn into the bathroom and he showed us how the burglars had got in.

A tiny window above the sink had been left open – the owners most likely reasoning that its small size, plus the iron bars over it, meant it was safe to do so. They were wrong. The window was wrenched out and the bars had been forced back, bent just far enough to allow a man – a small, skinny man – to squeeze through. The sink itself had been ripped from the wall, presumably unable to take the weight of the intruder as he climbed in. Behind the smashed porcelain, water trickled from a broken pipe, forming a pool around our feet.

We walked back to the front room, where a rucksack stuffed with electricals was placed on a chair by the door. 'See this here?' Steyn said, poking around with his torch, 'This is where they started packing. All this stuff they packed nicely – they thought they had enough time to take everything, but then they were disturbed.' He pointed to another chair, on which was stacked a DVD player, a stereo, what looked like a PlayStation. 'So they left all that stuff and the bag with all this stuff and just made off.'

Preparing to radio it in and let the robbery boys take over, he summed up the situation in his trademark style, no messing about and straight to the point, already eager to get on to whatever was going to happen next.

'There was a house break-in in progress. What happened was, there were two suspects on the premises and they were some- how disturbed and fled prior to our arrival. Like you saw, I took you in the house, all the stuff was all over the house; and as you saw the entry was through the bathroom window and they broke the sink so there's water all over the place. But it looks like they have disappeared without taking anything.'

He shrugged. 'So like I said you always have to be ready for anything.'

Steyn figured us unlucky to have missed the robbers, but we couldn't help feeling relieved. We'd seen the way he and his colleagues had gone in there – it was the second time we'd seen him and Chapman switch their safety catches off tonight already. Add to that Steyn's casual talk of 'deceasing' at least two men, as well as the enormous pool of blood we'd nearly stood in earlier, and it was beginning to seem like we were the only people in this country not carrying some sort of gun.

Which was not as much of a joke as it sounds. Nobody really knows how many illegal guns there are in South Africa, but esti- mates range between 500,000 and four million – as many as one for every 12 people.

Given all that, recovering illegal weapons is a massive task for the South African police. Most of them are stolen, and some come across the border from countries such as Mozambique and Zimbabwe – and by the time they hit the streets of Durban, an AK47 is going to cost you about the same as you'd pay for a DVD. It's little wonder everyone seems tooled up.

The robbery crime scene was duly handed over, but before we hit the road again, Steyn took a call on his mobile. 'Yeah?' he answered, before turning away from us and lowering his voice.

When the conversation was over, he beckoned his partner over and the two of them talked for a few minutes.

'Right,' he said, grinning as he jumped in the car and slammed the door shut, stashing the machine-gun by his feet. 'We're going to the station because there's an informer there. He's got information about stolen firearms. So we're gonna hear what his story is. Maybe take a couple of men in and hit the place.'

He nodded encouragingly. 'Maybe we will get some action later, eh? There's about five guns there, it could be a big draw. It will be dangerous. They got high-powered weapons, so anything can happen. They might hand them over, or they might try to fight. We will see.'

We asked him if these were illegal weapons. In other words, the type owned by criminals.

'That's it,' he said, grinning again, clearly the most excited he'd been all night. 'They're usually involved in attacks and gang warfare. Drugs. You never know what they might use these firearms for. That's why we arrest them.'

We took in the big policeman: his eyes were lit up like a kid's at Christmas. Finally, here was some proper action. As if everything so far had been run-of-the-mill ... He must have seen the look on our faces because he leant back and patted one of us reassuringly on the shoulder. 'Listen, I do worry sometimes, going into something like this. But you have to be professional. That's why we're going to talk to our man and plan it – so we can think of all that could happen.'

* * *

A couple hours later, the rendezvous in the underground car park was done and dusted, and we were set.

The informant had been pumped for all he had – and Steyn and his team were happy with what they heard. The nightclub was a favoured spot of car junkies, boy racers addicted to the adrenaline and danger of racing souped-up motors around town. They liked to meet at this place to burn off or stoke up a little energy – with drink, music, drugs, guns …

The clientele could wait, however. Tonight's raid was on the doormen, the guys providing security for the club. According to our mole they were not only carrying some pretty tasty ordnance, but their weapons were illegal.

It was a potentially lethal combination – and if the fight spread to those inside the club, the whole thing could blow up into a minor war. The Flying Squad did not want that to happen. They were going to go in hard and fast, wrap up the situation before anyone got brave, cocky, desperate or stupid.

In the back of Steyn and Chapman's car, we were so jumpy we could barely keep still. The clock was ticking round towards midnight and, as the city flashed by, every second brought the squad closer to what might be a major gunfight.

Calmly loading bullets into his machine-gun, Steyn confessed that, although as a young man it was exactly this feeling that he lived for, as he's got older he does take it a little easier. 'When I joined it was for the action,' he explained. 'No doubt. No second thoughts. But then you see other policeman getting killed and you think, you know, maybe it's not worth it. You think twice now. I've got a little son, he's two years and three months. It makes you think twice now about going to something.

'When I was younger I didn't care. But now … every single day I have to worry about him.'

But despite nearly 20 years on the force, Steyn is still no closer to understanding the extreme nature of crime in his country.

'Yes, I feel sorry for those that haven't got food and maybe steal bread,' he continues. 'But these hijackers – why do they have to shoot dead the person in the vehicle? For what? An innocent person who's got family, mum and dad or children. Why do you have to shoot them dead?

'With a cash in transit why do you have to burn the guard in the cash van? Why do they have to do that? ATM bombings, the police come and investigate and get shot in the head. Why do they have to do that?

'So I've got no sympathy for them,' he spat. 'Listen. If I get in a gunfight I'd fight my way out of it. As long as six or seven are dead I'll be happy. That's the way they want to be, they don't care. So then we don't care. That's how it goes.'

We were getting near the club now, and Steyn wanted to make it clear to us that if his attitude towards the bad guys seemed a little unforgiving, it's a lesson that's been learnt the hard way. And that he's still learning. He's done plenty of raids like this before … but every one is different. And every one has the potential to go tits up.

'It will be dangerous,' he stresses. 'They've got high-powered weapons, OK? Anything can happen there. They can hand them over or they might try and fight. Unfortunately in this job you can't make mistakes. It's not like a normal job. If you make a mistake, it could cost you your life.'

We pulled into a side street, the rest of the squad behind, and Steyn leant forward in his seat and shouldered his machine-gun. 'Turn those things off!' he hissed at Chapman, and we glided into a car park without headlights. The nightclub entrance was hidden behind a brick wall: Steyn wanted to give himself as much time as possible before his men were seen.

Silent as ghosts – albeit ghosts in blue and black body armour carrying machine-guns – the Flying Squad team moved quickly and efficiently towards the wall. And then, all of a sudden, with no warning, they were out and in the faces of the club doormen.

'Police!' barked Steyn, advancing steadily but with deceptive speed, the gun at his shoulder pointing squarely at the foremost security guard. He'd already spotted the danger man, the guy reaching for his own weapon. Tall and lanky, he was the security manager – and whether he was trying to impress his staff or he was just plain stupid wasn't clear. What was clear was that his first instinct when faced with a street full of heavily armed policemen was to go for his own weapon.

Big mistake.

'Put the gun down, put the gun down. Put the fucking gun down NOW!'

The man hesitated for a split second too long and Steyn was in his face. Behind him his two security staff were similarly caught in two minds, hands instinctively copying their boss and reaching for their weapons but, thankfully, brains engaging just enough to tell them not to even try it.

'Police!' shouted Steyn again, his barrel inches from the lead man now – who still hadn't let go of his own gun. 'Put it down! Down!'

Finally he did as he was told, and the others followed. 'Thank you,' said Steyn, with more than a touch of sarcasm. 'Now let me see your hands. Come around. Put your hands up. Listen to me.'

Unbelievably, the man was still holding out. 'For what?' he said, unable to hold the big cop's eye but jutting out his jaw and smirking like a surly child nonetheless. 'You've taken my gun.'

Steyn was in no mood for petulance: 'Put your hands up, put your hands up,' he repeated, the orders barked out like bursts of gunfire. 'Don't get clever. Raise your hands. Let me see your hands.'

The two men behind already had their arms pointed at the stars, but the manager was still smirking. One hand was stuck down the front of his trousers and Steyn wasn't liking it one bit. He jabbed his gun even closer. 'Put your hands up! Put your hands up! Listen to me! Put your hands up NOW.'

'Why?' he said, still unable to meet the cop's eye but not moving his hand nonetheless. 'You saw me, my gun's over there.' He nodded towards Chapman, who had a couple of LM5 automatic assault rifles on the floor in front of him.

Steyn was relentless. 'Put your hands up. Don't get clever.' His voice dropped – and if anything was even more intimidating than when he had been shouting. 'Listen to me for once. Put your hands up.'

Finally, the man saw sense – the moment his hand left his waistband Steyn was in there ... and pulled out a pistol.

He sighed. 'Don't get clever, my friend. You got a licence for these? I want to see your permits right now.'

There were no permits, and so the men were arrested and bundled into cars for further questioning at the station. But although things had gone as smoothly as he had hoped for, Steyn was still hyper-conscious of the club full of boy racers behind him – he didn't want anyone stumbling outside and trying to be a hero.

We left as we'd arrived – swiftly, silently, racing back into the night.

✾   ✾   ✾

Before signing off, Steyn debriefed us. The bust had been a success: they had recovered two LM5 automatic assault rifles, each with 30-round magazines locked and loaded, plus a 9mm pistol with around 15 rounds of ammunition. One of the LM5s was wanted in connection with a theft; the other, plus the pistol, were lacking proper certificates. Three deadly weapons and 75 rounds wasn't a bad haul – but what really made the bust a success was the fact that no shots had been fired, nobody had got hurt. No one tried to be a big man; all the cops got to go home at the end of their shifts.

'If they had put up a fight, there would have been a shootout,' he said. 'Of course we got them so quickly and by surprise it just stopped anything before it could happen. You never know, a shootout like that and innocent people can die, policemen can get injured, policemen can get killed, but the way we approached it I think was all right, it was fine. We were quick on them. They didn't know what to do.'

We couldn't help asking – the adrenaline, the thrill of the chase, facing down men with guns and taking out the bad guys … was that why he clocked on for work each day, put his life on the line in such extreme conditions? Or was it from a sense of duty to the people of Durban … or even to the supposed new South African dream?

'Yeah I do enjoy it, why not?' he shrugged. 'I enjoy this feeling … nice fast car, action, you know? And you can serve the public and help the public too – not all of it is swearing at them and trying to arrest them, you get nice people out there, people who are trying to help. You go to accidents, you try to help them.

'As for duty … well my duty is to protect and serve South African people. But not just South African people, any person who comes here and who wants to enjoy the scenery and the beauty of this country. I mean, any person who needs help or anything: that's what I do.'

The history of South Africa is writing itself so fast – making up for past wrongs, catching up with the decades lost to apartheid – that just keeping pace with the changes is a challenge. And as increasing numbers fail to adapt, some gulfs in society are widening – and crime is soaring. All of which makes the job of men like Andre Steyn a dizzying, exhausting race against time, with limited resources and numbers.

There's just too much happening out there. Too many guns, too many carjackings; too many murders, robberies, ATM jobs, cash in transit heists. Every night he's battling to keep on top of a crime epidemic – and every night he's putting his life on the line to do so.

We couldn't help being in awe of the guy.

'That's why so many policemen get stressed, because of all the scenes you see,' he told us. 'Sometimes it does affect you, but at the end of the day you just have to live with it. You wake up in the morning on your rest days, see your son, enjoy time with your family. That's where you go and relax, with your family and then when it comes to your shift, you have to be switched on again. That's the way it goes.

'Listen. This is who I am and this is what you see. As a policeman you can't hide anything. Everyone knows you. And this big chap' – cocking a thumb at Chapman – 'we've been partners for four years and we know exactly how each other works and it's like we're actually family. All policemen are like a close family, we all care for each other.'

He had one more point to make.

'What people say about South Africa may be true, but it is still a beautiful place. Yes, it can be dangerous being a policeman here, but you get problems all over the world. You should know that, right? The crime rate is high here, but at the end of the day it is still a beautiful place.'

He shook our hands, clapped the cameraman on the shoulder again and grinned. 'It's a beautiful place, bro. It's not all guns and carjackings. Go find the beach or something!'

WAR BABY:
NEJMA COLLACOVIC AND THE
FUTURE OF KOSOVO

Nejma Collacovic is not your usual cop. But then her patch – the fledgeling, war-torn state of Kosovo – is hardly the usual beat either. Ravaged by the worst excesses of the Balkan war at the end of the 1990s, it has never fully recovered. The United Nations moved in to protect Kosovo's citizens in 1999 – they're still there. And that same year, Europe's newest police force was formed: the Kosovo Police Service.

Nejma was in line at the recruiting station almost from the start – as a teenager, eager to make a difference. Even today, her passion remains undimmed.

In just about every other force we met around the world, it had always been about big men wielding big guns – men of huge experience who had put a lot of bad guys away … which was all great. But Kosovo is not your usual place – and we wanted to meet someone who didn't fit the usual mould.

This is such a new country, such a unique state – and in such a precarious position, politically, economically and socially – that somehow we couldn't help feeling the normal rules did not apply. If the Kosovo Police Service is to drag this country kicking and screaming into a safe, peaceful, crime-free future, someone's going to have to come along and give the place something it's never seen before.

We found that someone. She's got great cheekbones – and she's lethal with an MP5.

✵   ✵   ✵

THE FIRING RANGE on the outskirts of Pristina is not an easy place to get near. For a start there are no signposts. Or buildings. Only a dusty, pot-holed track leading into the scrubby hills and the near-constant rat-a-tat of live gunfire to guide you in.

The sound of shooting comes with a lot of bad memories here. Recent memories, too.

Once you reach the end of the track and are pulled up by the group of vans, 4x4s, targets and sandbags that make up the range, the noise just gets louder. We parked up and made our way towards a group of officers from the Kosovo Police Service, here to sharpen their skills before resuming the daily battle for the streets of this tiny country.

As we watched, one of them sauntered up to the targets, pistol held firmly, easily, in both hands. Despite the standard-issue uniform, the black combats and boots, the bulky bullet-proof top and the beret pulled low, something about this particular officer stood out. This cop wasn't like the others. This cop was a girl.

Suddenly she dropped to her knee, loosed a couple of shots into the nearest human-shaped target, before rolling once to her right, squeezing off another, then rolling again to her left and firing again. Finally, flat on her back, she held the gun over her head and emptied the clip behind her – effectively firing blind.

There was a moment's silence as, still lying on the ground, she checked her weapon, holstered it and got to her feet. And then everyone started applauding.

This girl was good. More than that – she was lethal. Those were the kind of tricks you see in the movies: we didn't think people actually did that rolling on your back and shooting thing in real life.

The girl herself looked up, as if noticing everyone else for the first time, before shooting the gallery a quick smile and going to retrieve her target.

'Who is she?' we asked. The instructor who had escorted us from the car to the range smiled. 'Nejma Collacovic,' he said simply, and, motioned for us to follow as he joined her. She was studying her target, inspecting her work. It was peppered with holes – all of them in and around the two smallest circles: the area between the stomach and neck. The kill zone.

'The tactic is to shoot fast. Don't fear, shoot fast,' she explained. 'The best shots are here in this region: the centre of the mass, that's what we aim for, this here.' She indicated the small area in which all of her bullets had made Swiss cheese of the target. 'This is the fatal zone. We use firearms as a last resort – but when we do all police officers are obliged to shoot at the centre of the suspect.'

But Nejma wasn't done yet. New targets were put up, and walking back towards the firing line, she tightened her gloves and rolled up her sleeves, revealing long, tanned, slim arms – before hefting an MP5 machine-gun and checking the magazine.

'This is the MP5 automatic gun that our unit uses,' she said. 'We use it in training and in real conditions. They are semi-automatic, 9mm calibre and have three ways of shooting. The first way is one by one bullet, the second way is three bullets at once and the third way is ... it unloads all of the bullets at once.'

She smiled again, and this time there was a glint of mischief in her eye. Up close we could see that she was younger than most of the other cops we had met around the world – she couldn't even have been out of her twenties yet.

'It's a very adaptable and professional weapon,' she said, motioning for us to stand well back. 'They are very suitable, very precise, very nice equipment that we have.'

Glancing quickly around to make sure everyone was clear, she crouched, squeezed the trigger and let off a burst. Even at our distance we could see the holes ripped in the target – and the sprays of dirt kicked up in the hillside 100 feet behind. Those were real bullets: and Nejma was tearing the living daylights out of whatever she aimed them at.

We hadn't come to Kosovo to meet Nejma Collacovic, but we had to talk more with her.

※　※　※

When the production company was drawing up a shortlist of places to visit in search of the world's toughest cops, Kosovo had been a dead cert from the start. It turned out to be the only European country we visited.

We even knew what it was we wanted. After all, Kosovo's problems are not exactly hidden from the world.

With a population of just over two million, Kosovo is one of the smallest regions in the Balkans. But it is also one of the most volatile. Located on the Balkan Peninsula, in the south-east of Europe, it borders Montenegro, Albania, Macedonia and Serbia, and, at one time or another, just about everyone has wanted a piece of it.

It is one of the most war-torn territories in the world – invaded throughout its history time and time again. It has been part of the Roman, Byzantine, Bulgarian and Serbian empires, and in 1389 it became part of the Ottoman Empire – establishing close ties with the Middle East, and introducing Islam to the population.

But the real trouble has come far more recently.

In the late 1990s Kosovo was ripped apart again when it became involved in the deadly Balkan war. The states that made up the former Yugoslavia disintegrated into a bloody, hate-fuelled conflict that tore up the whole region along ethnic lines. In the middle of it all was Kosovo – part Serb, part Albanian.

KOSOVO

As Serbs and Kosovo Albanians fought a violent battle for control of Kosovo, more than a million ethnic Albanians fled or were forcibly driven from the region and over 10,000 people were killed. Many of the dead were victims of ethnic cleansing as the Serbs brought a brutal new dimension to their attempts to overpower the Kosovo Albanians.

The conflict was ended in 1999 when NATO intervened, bombing the Serbs into submission in a bid to end the genocide. The United Nations moved in to police the area, where tensions between the two groups still raged ... and still simmer today.

The war here is officially over: but five minutes on Google will tell you that not everyone follows the party line. Serbs and Albanians still clash on the streets; the UN still has its hands full just trying to keep the native Kosovars from tearing each other apart again. We had been set up to meet one of those trying to prevent another all-out war: regional commander of the UN police in the divided city of Mitrovica, Scotsman David McLean.

But his was never going to be the full story. Away from the political and ethnic struggle for control of the state, Kosovo is being invaded again.

Into the breach left by the fallout of the Kosovo war at the turn of the millennium, came the criminal underworld. Like predators sensing an easy kill, they moved fast ... exploiting the political instability and lack of proper policing and establishing Kosovo as a base for their lucrative trade. In less than a decade, the country has been flooded with drugs, guns and prostitution. Its flimsy borders and key position as a link in the smuggling route from Afghanistan to the West means Kosovo now sees an estimated 5000 kilos of heroin pass through its streets every month – that's around 40 per cent of the world's total heroin supply.

As if that wasn't enough to deal with, trafficking women for prostitution has become big business in Kosovo.

This place is seen as an easy target. It has over 700 miles of border and strong criminal links to the Eastern European countries, where the victims are often seduced by the promise of an EU passport, kidnapped and forced to work in Kosovo brothels to 'earn' their passage to the West. There are an estimated 25,000 women trafficked through the Balkans every year: and they are bought and sold for as little as £600.

If £600 seems cheap for a life, it is. But do the maths. That much money multiplied by that many women adds up to £15 million a year.

And then there are the guns. As might be expected in a country that was at the centre of a desperate and bloody war just a decade ago, the streets are loaded with guns. When the official shooting stopped not everyone was so keen to turn over the weapons that had kept them alive thus far. There are reckoned to be up to 400,000 small arms in Kosovo – or roughly one for every five people, man, woman and child – and the United Nations have said that 70 per cent of households own at least one firearm.

It's a big old mess. And trying to clear it up, with some help from the UN, is the Kosovo Police Service: so new it's practically still wet behind the ears.

We'd come to meet the new peacemakers. The law enforcers fighting a new war – a war against an international invading army, consisting of criminals of every nationality, intent on flooding the country with drugs, guns and prostitution. It's a battle that would test the most experienced forces – so how could a rookie outfit like the KPS cope?

We wanted to find out. But what we didn't expect was to discover a slim, softly spoken girl in her twenties at the heart of it all.

KOSOVO

✵   ✵   ✵

Before we left the shooting range we cornered Nejma. She was shy at first, wary of us, a bit embarrassed as to why we should be at all interested in talking to her. We weren't sure ourselves – but after what we had seen we figured it was at least worth a chat. As she warmed up it turned out, as we had guessed, that Nejma wasn't just another ordinary cop.

Nejma was 27 years old, and had been part of the Kosovo Police Service from almost as soon as it was formed after the war in 1999. In that time she had risen through the ranks from raw recruit to lead a unit of 29 men.

This was her team at the shooting range, here as part of their regular training. They need to stay razor sharp: they were set up to tackle the heavily armed criminals who see Kosovo as an easy target.

'Yes, these are my men,' she said, removing her beret and smoothing her hair. 'Today we came here to train: we shoot with our everyday guns, small guns, and we also train with the MP5 automatic rifles. Even though we don't have enough equipment, we have to do it at least once every two weeks for our unit to stay alert and ready. It would be very good if all the police officers could do this training, but because of the fact that our unit has this equipment, we're lucky enough to be able to do it.'

So is a lack of equipment an issue for the police here?

'Sure,' she shrugged. 'Yes, it is a problem that we don't have enough equipment, and most of the time we suffer for it … but either way we are proud to do our duty even with this small amount of equipment that we do have. And,' she smiled again, 'we always achieve our goal on time.

'All jobs and all professions have to begin somewhere and we're no different. And it's more important for us because Kosovo is a place that in a small period of time has became a state, and it's necessary to have the knowledge about our weapons: the usage and the conditions of using them, when to use them, how to use them. As I said in the beginning, we train with our pistols, the 9mm small arms – all the police force of Kosovo are equipped with those; but our unit is also equipped with automatic machine-guns.'

Njema's unit train hard, week in, week out, because they know from bitter experience that any operation could be their last. Recently one of their number was killed while involved in an operation to take down one of the criminal gangs. It still hurts.

'My colleague, Triumf, lost his life on duty,' Nejma told us, feet planted apart and hands defiantly hooked into her bullet-proof vest. 'He was one of the best officers in Kosovo but on this occasion, and thanks to what happened that day, the criminals achieved their aim and killed him on duty. I still feel bad. When he died I felt like I had lost a part of me.'

But even though she has seen one of her close friends killed in the line of duty, her resolve has not wavered.

'I'm a policewoman because I love this profession and it has become part of my life. I also feel that I owe this country and its people to serve them.'

That sense of duty has its roots in the war itself. Nejma was just 17 when her country fell apart – and those years left some deep scars for her personally. Her 22-year-old brother was killed in the fighting, and her father was shot and taken prisoner.

'Just like any everyone else we tried to cope but it was very difficult,' she told us. 'A lot of things happened to my family during the war. My father was put in the military prison in Montenegro.

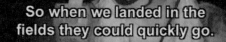
So when we landed in the fields they could quickly go.

TOP LEFT COPES commando John Orejuela: his friendly attitude and easy-going, open features hide a seriously dedicated professionalism.
TOP RIGHT Terrorist raids in the pitch black of the Colombian bush.
ABOVE Flying over the jungle – the choppers are armed with GAU-17 mini-guns, capable of spraying the trees with 50 rounds a second.

NEXT PAGE
TOP Juliet Quintero, aka Nikita – elite sniper with the Colombian anti-kidnapping unit.
MIDDLE RIGHT 'This didn't feel much like policing. This felt like... Apocalypse Now.'
MIDDLE LEFT Colonel Chavarro's men take out another cocaine lab – this one alone was capable of producing £45 million of coke a month.
BOTTOM Racing back to the Black Hawk helicopter before the terrorist cartels can regroup for a counter-attack.

TOP On-the-job briefings with a member of the New Orleans VOWS unit. These boys deal with everything from tactical assaults and SWAT raids to cruising the city's worst areas on the look-out for trouble.

ABOVE Feeling good after helping take down my first suspect.

TOP Officer Jeff Roach, the VOWS unit prize fighter, fails to be intimidated by the prospect of facing me in the ring.

ABOVE LEFT The boys pile out of the Bear Cat and storm the house of a murder suspect. We were told to keep our distance on this one.

ABOVE RIGHT Dance like a butterfly, sting like a ... butterfly.

..it could cost you your life.

TOP LEFT Andre Steyn reminds us why failing to follow his orders would be a bad idea.
TOP RIGHT Steyn advances on suspects outside a nightclub: 'If they had put up a fight there would have been a shootout.'
ABOVE There aren't many men I'd want beside me in the trenches – but I'd want Andre Steyn.

TOP LEFT Nejma Collacovic: lethal with an MP5.

TOP RIGHT The Kosovo Police Service on manoeuvres: barely a decade old and fighting a crime invasion.

ABOVE The Department Against Organised Crime raid a suspect house – and smash an international drugs gang.

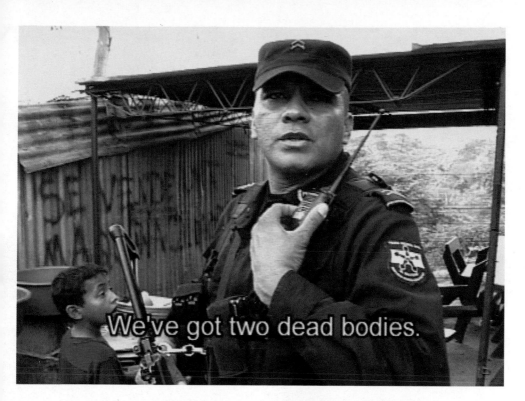

We've got two dead bodies.

TOP Captain Umberto Flores Aragon of the El Salvador Inteceptores gets exactly the kind of action he warned us about.
LEFT Before the murder, most of the day had been spent busting gang members in San Salvador.
ABOVE Shot point blank in the face – we were there within minutes.

The prison was called Spuz. He was locked up there until October 1999 when we had to pay to bail him out and buy his freedom. I find it very difficult to talk about anything and everything that happened to me and my family during the war. Unfortunately, you need to be part of a war to understand what it's actually all about. I could write a book about all the nightmares that happened to me and all of us during these horrific times.'

At the first opportunity she had after the ceasefire, Nejma enrolled in the KPS. 'The very first motive was the Kosovo war itself,' she admits. 'My motive was to serve the people of Kosovo. I want to try to help them to gain a freedom they deserved as I didn't have it in my childhood.'

As for the fact that she's a woman – she smiled at our question, but batted it away easily. 'Yes, most of the time it gets people's attention,' she said, 'and most of the time the people don't look towards women as authority figures – and that's probably because before, during the times of the former Yugoslavia, there simply weren't any policewomen. And so no citizens in Kosovo have ever had experience dealing with policewomen.'

She shrugged. 'I'm proud to be a woman leading this unit of men and I think their actions show that they're proud to be led by me.'

We left the shooting range with the sound of gunfire – and the echo of her words – still ringing in our ears.

✳   ✳   ✳

The Kosovo Police Service was set up after the war under the guidance of the United Nations. If this country is to ever recover from the horrors of its recent history and become anything like a peaceful, Western democracy, then the police force are fundamental to that process. But they're right up against it. We'd already heard about one dead officer: another 10 have met violent deaths in the KPS since it was established. Cops here are 50 times more likely to be killed violently than in the UK.

We had been scheduled to meet three of the men fighting to bring some order to this struggling new nation – fighting, it has to be said, against the weight of both ancient prejudices and ruthlessly modern criminal techniques. As well as hooking up with David McLean of the United Nations police in the troubled city of Mitrovica, we were to go out with Ramadan Ahmeti of the anti-trafficking unit as they busted a brothel used for illegal prostitution. First, however, we were to meet Major Haxhi Kraniqi, deputy chief of the newly formed Department Against Organised Crime.

They are a specialist unit set up to combat the increasingly influential underworld who are exploiting Kosovo's weak borders and shaky security, and using this place as a base from which to enter Europe. Haxhi and his team are on the front line in the fight against these ruthless gangs – combating men dealing in massive amounts of drugs and guns.

We met him at police HQ as his squad were preparing for a raid on a gang he suspected were involved in a large heroin deal. Everyone was suited and booted, in black and dark blue, wrapped in combat vests, wielding MP5s. These weren't a regular troop of officers: for a special op like this, Haxhi is able to cherry-pick, calling on elite officers from across the KPS – guys who are trained to deal with the most dangerous criminals. As we watched they saluted smartly and loaded into a fleet of 4x4s.

Haxhi was not going with them – not just yet. His days of front-line action are not as frequent as they used to be: now, as befits a major, he's more often the man masterminding the raids, rather than the cop busting down the doors and leading the team in.

He didn't look much like a door-busting type, to be honest. Friendly, polite, with excellent English, he was also very smart for a cop: clean shaven, with a well-pressed uniform and impeccably ironed shirt. He was clearly management; he had the air of a man used to dealing with the politics of law enforcement as much as the daily reality of it.

In football he'd be a chairman rather than one of the boot-room staff – albeit a chairman with the ear and the trust of his players, but someone pulling the strings from on high. In the movie game he'd be one of those 'executive producer' guys who come on set to either praise or bollock the crew.

But his status didn't mean he planned to stay in the office all afternoon. His men were under strict instructions to keep him in the loop – and as soon as there was word of a result, one way or the other, he'd be joining them.

Management class he may be, but Haxhi shared something with every serving cop we met in Kosovo – a deep, passionate, patriotic love of their country, and a burning desire to do whatever it took to make it a better place. 'Fighting organised crime – it's something special,' he told us. 'Because we know we are doing this job to serve our people. To help Kosovo to be without narcotics. This is high motivation.'

When the call came in, he was already in the car, tensed, waiting. He listened … and then he smiled, turned the key and fired it up. He'd got a result. His team had raided a house in a remote village 20 miles outside the capital – and had overpowered the gang members inside and seized a quantity of uncut heroin, still wrapped, still in the shoebox-sized bricks in which they'd been transported into this country.

As he drove, he talked, phone pressed to his ear. There were only three questions: How many arrests? How much heroin? How many shots fired?

The answers were all good. Two men had been arrested without a shot being fired: one had been hiding in the attic, the other made a run for it – he was persuaded to come down from the roof of the building by seven or eight officers pointing semi-automatic machine-guns at him. And as for the drugs … there was a lot. A huge amount, in fact.

'They found more than 10 kilos,' he grinned, slapping the steering wheel. 'They said around 10 to 15 kilos, but we will learn when we arrive there … and as for the arrests, the suspects are mixed – a Turkish citizen and a Kosovar.'

By the time we arrived, the information had just got better. The Kosovo Police Service had just struck gold. 'What can I say?' he grinned. 'I'm feeling very well. The complete gang were arrested and we have more than 15 kilos, somewhere around 20 kilos of heroin.'

Haxhi's operation had busted an international crime gang and seized heroin with a UK street value of over a million quid. The gang members would be looking at up to 10 years in prison, a huge success in the KPS's fight against organised crime.

'The amount of narcotics is not the big issue for the judges,' he said. 'You have to prove this is an organised crime network. But in this instance, sure it was. We have here a Turkish citizen arrested, we have the people who sell the narcotics, we have the people who buy the narcotics.'

Haxhi saved his final flourish for his jubilant troops. Holding up his phone, he addressed them all, quoting from the screen. 'I'll read you a text message I've just got from the Home Secretary,' he said. 'He speaks for the whole government of Kosovo. "Please give everyone my thanks and support. Congratulations to every-one that made this a successful operation." That was from the minister. I personally congratulate you too.'

✻   ✻   ✻

Next up was Ramadan Ahmeti of the anti-trafficking unit. A bit rougher round the edges than Haxhi, Ramadan didn't even wear a uniform, let alone a perfectly ironed one. When we met him he was in plain clothes: a slightly dishevelled suit and rumpled, open-necked shirt. And if he looked harassed, that's because he was. Ramadan deals in dangerous situations, sure: but he also deals in tragedy. You can see it in his eyes. When cops bust heroin dealers, or gun-runners, the victims of those crimes remain anonymous, unseen – all the cops see is the prize, the stash, captured before it gets to the people whose life it ruins. And once they've found that stash, they seize it, destroy it, congratulate themselves and go home happy.

But in a unit like Ramadan's the target is the victims themselves. The stash they're after is human. He's not taking out packages of heroin … he's rescuing real human beings. And that's got to get to you after a while.

Ramadan heads a unit that is responsible for stemming one of the region's fastest growing problems – human trafficking.

Trafficking people for prostitution has become big business in Kosovo. And for the organised crime gangs, there is big money to be made. In the town of Ferizaj, half way between Pristina and the Macedonian border, we met Ramadan and his unit as they headed out on a night raid. They were closing in on a bar they suspected to be operating as an illegal brothel. Their information had it that a Serbian woman was being held there – forced into sex with punters against her will.

'We believe that she is a victim of trafficking which is used for prostitution,' he told us. 'I'm feeling good because I know that in the end I will save the life of someone that really needs to be saved. When I see the victims, especially when they are minors, I think to myself, what if she was my daughter or my sister? We have to fight against the criminals and save the good people.'

The raid, when it happened, did not have the drama and fire-works of other ops we'd been on – there were no machine-guns, no helicopters; they weren't expecting serious armed resistance. Ramadan's cops had guns – but they were sidearms only, and for the most part kept holstered. Nevertheless, raids like this still carry a risk for the cops. There's always the chance something will go wrong.

'This is a dangerous job,' he told us, moments before he led his men in, 'because you are dealing with criminals. Organised crime is more difficult and dangerous than other types of crime. If I will be killed or shot I will be afraid at the time … but until then I have to work.'

And with that his men were in, moving efficiently through the building with truncheons and handguns, quickly isolating the danger man – in this case the bar owner – and sealing the place against any threat. Once he had been apprehended, it was a just a case of finding the girl.

She was upstairs, half-dressed, in a shabby room with only a dirty bed and a collapsing wardrobe for company. She was pretty too – beautiful even, with those East European high cheekbones and dark eyes. But she burst into tears when the cops came in, and hid her head. She did not choose this – she had been brought here from Serbia against her will, and once the bar owner had taken her ID card from her, she was trapped. Her tears were part relief – and part shame.

'The girl is going to be taken back to the shelter we have,' Ramadan said. 'It looks in her eye that she is happy that we are here.'

He smiled – and his smile had sadness around the edges. The fact that the girl was Serbian, the country responsible for the slaughter of so many Kosovo Albanians like him barely a decade before, did not matter to Ramadan. Freeing her was just part of his job. 'She's a Serbian and I am happy we're serving all people, no matter their nationality or religion or background,' he said. 'I am happy just to fight this crime, to try to make a better future for our people; for all our daughters and our sons.'

✣　　✣　　✣

Ramadan's attitude, sadly, is not shared by all of Kosovo's population. In the town of Mitrovica, 30 miles north-east of the capital and close to the Serbian border, the United Nations police are still out in numbers, desperately trying to maintain some kind of peace.

Mitrovica is a town at war with itself. In the south of the city live the Kosovo Albanians, and in the north the Kosovo Serbs. Both groups still see Mitrovica – and Kosovo itself – as their territory. Many of them are prepared to fight for it.

The man charged with keeping the peace in this hotspot is Scotsman David McLean. As regional commander of the UN police in Mitrovica, David knows the city better than most.

'Mitrovica's like a modern-day Northern Ireland,' he told us. 'Murders are quite common: we had one last week, we've had one today. This is just normal daily policing for this region.'

Older than either Haxhi or Ramadan, David comes across as a solid, straight-down-the-line kind of bloke. Although when we met him he was behind the wheel of a UN car with a holstered pistol at his side, it wasn't difficult to imagine him in the stands at the footy on a Saturday afternoon with his kids, or sharing a quiet drink with some mates in the pub afterwards. His hair was close-cropped and greying, he had a bit of a paunch developing – but his eyes had a twinkle to them.

David joined the British MoD police in 1991. He volunteered for his UN posting in Kosovo in June 2007. And despite having worked around the globe, he's never seen anything quite like Mitrovica. 'The weapons that we come under attack from are mostly AK47s: very powerful. If you go through all the history since we arrived in '99, I think nearly every household in Kosovo has had one of these in them at one time, and many still have at this present time. The violence can erupt at any second.'

And when it does it's the KPS and the UN who get caught in the middle of it. They often come under fire simply trying to keep the Kosovo Serbs and Kosovo Albanians apart.

David has policed some of the most violent clashes that Mitrovica has ever seen: he described one of the worst, in March 2008.

Kosovo had recently declared itself an independent state, no longer under UN administration. This provoked a violent response from the Kosovo Serbs, who fervently believe that Kosovo is a province of Serbia. In protest at the declaration, Kosovo Serb court workers broke into the city's courthouse and staged a sit-in.

The events of that day are stamped on David's mind.

'The court workers broke off the fence gates,' he told us. 'There was a crowd of maybe 300 of them, they forced their way past the gates and then broke in through the window.' They stayed in the courthouse for three full days before, feeling their point made, they agreed to leave peacefully with the police. That was when the trouble really started.

'Once they were taken into detention they were put into prison escort vehicles and they were taken out by the rear gate,' he continued. 'But when they proceeded out through the rear, the vehicles came under attack.' A huge mob had gathered in support of the original protestors – and they didn't like seeing them carried off as prisoners. Their anger turned on the authorities. The situation quickly descended into chaos.

'One of the UN vehicles was actually burnt,' said David. 'A bus was set on fire … What they were doing was they were using a petrol station just across the square to make their Molotov cock-tails. They were rolling up with crates of bottles, just filling them with petrol, putting cloth into them and just throwing them constantly.'

The mob succeeded in freeing the protestors and then attacked with renewed ferocity. 'We came under attack from AK47s, mortars, hand grenades thrown at the front gate, more thrown at the back gate. We had mortar attacks coming in above us … It was a war zone.'

By the time it was over the police had lost one officer and 63 others lay injured. The dead man was a colleague of David's. 'Officer Ihor from Ukraine was subject to a hand grenade attack,' he said simply. 'Knowing that it was a fellow officer hurts you. You think to yourself: is there anything I could have done better to improve things? Who was to blame? Can I find a culprit that carried that out? And that's my main aim at the moment – to make sure that a thorough investigation is carried out.'

Despite the risks, the danger doesn't faze David. In fact, he relishes it. 'My job's a hobby to me,' he explained, 'ever since I joined the police way back in 1991. Each day I do it because I love it. Believe it or not, it's a buzz.

'Back home I have a wife and three children and I'm missing out on some of the most important times of their life – coming up to doing higher education and all that. Sometimes I think to myself, am I selfish being here? Should I be back home with them? But who else is going to come and do this job? I put my heart into this job.'

We liked David a lot. We liked Haxhi and Ramadan too – and as well as liking them we admired all these men, admired their dedication, courage and the sacrifices they were making in pursuit of a better Kosovo. They were all, in their own way, extraordinary cops.

But we couldn't get the girl off our minds. The achievements so far of Nejma Collacovic might not look as impressive on paper … but there was something about her. Something important. We had to see her again.

✹   ✹   ✹

As it turned out, Nejma's unit were training for a mission in the town of Peja, in an area of Kosovo known as the Wild West because of its history of gun fights.

Situated near the borders of both Montenegro and Albania, the region is a key point for smugglers – they ferry in guns, drugs, cigarettes and girls in huge quantities, as if they're daring the authorities to try to stop them – and the lack of any real local economy means that Peja has become a battleground for powerful criminal gangs intent on protecting their own interests at any cost.

As well as smuggling, these gangs are involved in protection rackets, kidnapping and extortion. There was even one scheme where they took illegal possession of homes that Albanians had bought from departing Serbs – and then demanded a payout to leave.

With so many gangs operating in the area, turf wars are common – and innocent civilians are often caught in the crossfire. In August 2003, three people, including two girls aged 11 and 14, were murdered when attackers sprayed a car with bullets on a busy street in broad daylight. No one was ever arrested. A week later another man died and two men were injured when their vehicle was ambushed nearby: again, a dispute between the gangs was blamed.

For the KPS, Peja is a nightmare. For Nejma, it's a problem she intended to start sorting. First she needed to get her young, inexperienced team up to speed. That night she was leading a training exercise … learning how to track and apprehend a suspect vehicle carrying highly dangerous suspects involved in organised crime. It may only have been practice, but the lessons learnt could save their lives. So they were playing it for real.

We met her unit as she briefed them.

They were assembled in a room in the police HQ, sitting attentively around a long table. Nejma herself was at the head of the table, a whiteboard behind her, a couple of weighty-looking ring binders in front of her. Along both sides of the room were gleaming rows of lockers. In contrast to some of the stations we had visited around the world, everything seemed clean, well-ordered, new. We had to remind ourselves: that's because it was new. This was a new police force – and Nejma's squad were a brand new unit inside it.

The mood was relaxed – this was to be a training exercise, after all – but Nejma maintained a calm authority. She may have been the only woman in a room full of big men … but there was no doubting that she was in charge. The unit listened to her every word; she didn't need to raise her voice once.

'OK,' she started, and everyone immediately fell silent. 'Tonight there will be an operation acting on information from the Regional Investigation Unit. A suspect is expected to enter the territory of Kosovo. We believe that this person has committed many serious crimes, such as human trafficking, guns smuggling, and he is suspected for a murder.

'That person will be stopped by us on the road to Peja. We are going to arrest the suspect and we'll bring him to the base where other procedures will take place, in accordance to the law. There are 13 police officers involved tonight. Each one of you is familiar with your duties and you know what kind of responsibilities you have, how you are going to get the job done.

'We will be operating with full equipment.'

There followed a series of questions on the finer points of the operation, and after a few more minutes, the ring binder was snapped shut and everyone stood up. As we watched, the men hit the lockers and started to load up.

Dozens of straps and fastenings were buckled and clipped, bags and utility belts and pouches secured, torches and hand-cuffs and earpieces slotted into place. Bullet-proof vests were shrugged on and tied tight, berets firmly positioned … and, last of all, the weapons were checked and double-checked. Pistols in holsters, MP5s strapped over their shoulders. They were ready.

'All of this equipment is necessary because of the nature of the suspect we are going to take down,' Nejma told us. 'First of all it's for personal safety because the operation which is about to take place is considered high risk and also it's for the protection of the citizens.'

We asked her how she felt when she was getting ready for something like this.

Nejma smiled that half-shy, half-defiant smile again, the same one we had seen on the training ground after she wasted the targets.

'I feel very happy and very proud,' she said. 'I feel proud because I'm serving this country. I am very proud of my seven years' experience serving the people of Kosovo.'

* * *

We didn't know what to make of it all. The operation itself was a success ... but at the end of the day, it was just a training exercise. The guns were not loaded with live ammo. And even if Nejma and her team were playing it for real, the inescapable fact remained that the 'suspect' was not a gun-running murderer at all, but actually one of her team acting out a role.

Which is not to say the whole thing didn't go down well. It was done brilliantly, expertly: the suspect's car ambushed, forced to stop, the man himself restrained and detained in seconds, bundled into the police car and whisked back to the station with a minimum amount of opportunity for trouble. Nejma herself led the operation like a seasoned pro, coordinating her men and taking down the suspect herself.

It was impressive ... but it wasn't real. It was training.

But then perhaps we were just being impatient. The whole point about Nejma Collacovic was that she was different from the other cops we'd met. She was young, keen, sharp ... but her career in the force was also as old as the KPS itself. She joined at the beginning, got in there as a teenager, desperate to make a difference. And in just seven years she'd risen from raw recruit to the leader of a brand new unit of 29 men. She had, as someone once put it, the right stuff.

And if Kosovo is ever going to free itself of its bloody history and its chaotic present, it's going to be people like Nejma who make it happen.

Watching her as she led her men through the operation, calmly ordering them to their positions, taking control of the situation, keeping everyone together and disciplined and always with one eye on the bigger picture, we couldn't help being impressed. She's a born leader, this girl. And she's driven by something more than just a love of the action.

Nejma hadn't given us the adrenaline or the headlines, she hadn't impressed us with stories of the war, high-profile busts or even text messages from the government ... but she did represent something altogether more important. This young Kosovo Albanian girl with the steady eyes, the lethal shot and the quick, shy smile represents the future of the Kosovo Police Service. In a funny way, she's the future of this country.

'My team – they all feel like a family and I consider them as family members,' she told us on the way back to the base. 'When I have a day off I actually feel quite bored. I feel very bad and I miss these officers I work with. I love this work and the Kosovo police is a very important part of my life. I live for my job.

'You must be prepared 24 hours a day as a police officer,' she continued, leaning forward in the car, her eyes locked on to us, her stare intense. 'You must accept the job as part of your life. Why? Because it is necessary for this country. And if you love the job with all your heart, then you will serve the people with all your heart. You have to be ready to help people all the time, any time. Being in the Kosovo police is part of your life.

KOSOVO

'During my job and the seven years that I have experienced in the Kosovo Police Service, I have never had a situation where I was frightened or felt sorry for someone that has not obeyed the law. I do nothing more than serve this country.'

GANGSTER TRIPPIN':
ON THE STREETS WITH UMBERTO
FLORES ARAGON

El Salvador – a country named after Jesus Christ. Its name means 'The Saviour', but for some here, it's a living hell.

Gangs have torn this place in two, the bitter legacy of a bloody civil war. Everyone is affected: and those who aren't running with the gangs are living in constant fear of them.

The besieged, outmanned, outgunned police force is struggling to stem the tide of violence – every month another cop is killed trying to keep the peace. Traditional methods no longer work: and so a new unit has been created. The Inteceptores.

This elite squad is headed by Captain Umberto Flores Aragon, a cool-as-ice veteran who grew up in the ghettos and who in 16 years in the force has seen it all and done it all. Umberto tells it like it is and doesn't care who hears it – and his unswerving passion for protecting El Salvador's citizens inspires a fierce devotion amongst his men … and fear in the nation's criminals.

We hit the streets with Umberto and his men. We had no brief, no agenda, no steers on what we wanted to see. And what we got was simple: no distractions, no frills, no messing around. Just one day with the Inteceptores.

It began with a warning – and it ended in murder.

✥   ✥   ✥

CAPTAIN UMBERTO FLORES ARAGON was trying to make something clear to us.

'Don't leave this car without me,' he warned, leaning on the bonnet, one finger raised and his eyes locked steady. Behind him, members of his team, dressed identically in black combats and boots, black bullet-proof vests, black baseball caps, loaded themselves into a pick-up. Two in the front, three in the back, machine-guns ready.

'In this area, if someone from the outside comes here, there is a 75 to 100 per cent chance that they will leave again – but without their possessions,' he continued. 'They might even leave with their car, but never with the goods still inside. Round here, suddenly they'll come out of their houses, everyone at once. They'll rob you quickly and then disappear again. And that's if you're lucky. Otherwise you could end up dead.'

Umberto heads up the Inteceptores, a nine-man crack squad charged with special ops in the streets of El Salvador. And, more often than not, that means gang control.

This country is being torn apart by gangs. For years the two biggest have been at war. Mara Salvatrucha – or MS – and 18th Street have carved up the place between them. In some areas they live just streets apart, and if their own territories are off-limits to outsiders, the no-man's-lands between them can be killing fields. Anyone is fair game – and with business interests including drugs, armed robbery, extortion and kidnapping, protecting their turf means doing whatever it takes. Including murder.

But everywhere has gangs, right? Sure. But not like they do here. The situation's got so bad that the government has taken the most extreme action possible: after the violence threatened to destroy the country completely, they've come down hard. Gang membership has been criminalised – in modern El Salvador you don't even have to be actively involved in gang activities to be breaking the law. Simply being a member of a gang, or even associating with gang members, is now illegal.

And that's where Captain Umberto and the Inteceptores come in. Formed just 15 months before we arrived in El Salvador, they're the latest police weapon in the war against the gangs. And if they have a seriously cool name … well they're a seriously cool outfit.

Coolest of them all is Umberto. He even looks a bit like George Clooney: fortyish, tall and solid, he's also thoughtful, deliberate and careful with his words. There's a kind of restrained power there as well, like he could cut loose at any moment. We'd see for ourselves just how.

The nine-man Inteceptores team are brimming with confidence too. They're in love with their jobs – and half in love with themselves. They know they're the best of the best: most pimp up their all-black military-style uniform with wraparound shades, wearing their baseball caps pulled low.

There's a genuine camaraderie amongst these men, a do-anything-for-each-other attitude born of shared danger. The Inteceptores trust each other with their lives. They have to: it's what they do every time they lace up their boots, pick up their guns and go to work.

And it's obvious to anyone that all his men worship Captain Umberto. He's the one they'd follow through the gates of hell if necessary. Sometimes it feels like they're doing exactly that.

We were with the Inteceptores for a single day. It was supposed to be a pretty standard shift: chasing gang members, tracking down suspects and seeing what else turned up. Umberto himself was in optimistic mood.

'Hopefully we'll get something today,' he said, winking as the squad loaded up and got ready to roll. 'A bit of action for you.'

We wanted to know: do you like action?

The reply came after a few moments' thought, accompanied by a slow grin. 'Yes. I do quite like my action,' he said. Behind him, waiting in the pick-up, machine-guns resting casually on their knees, a couple of his men laughed.

We'd get action all right. At that time we had no idea what kind.

❉   ❉   ❉

El Salvador's out-of-control gang culture has its roots in blood and revolution.

For most of the last century, this country was run with an iron fist by a military-backed government, with a few wealthy families getting super-rich on the back of the vast majority of under-class workers. Uprisings were ruthlessly dealt with: in 1932 a Communist-led peasant rebellion ended in the slaughter of 25,000 people – a crackdown they now call La Matanza, or the Massacre.

In 1979 the people had finally had enough and full-scale civil war broke out. For 12 long and brutal years the extreme right-wing government, funded by the United States, and a coalition of left-wing guerrilla groups known as the FMLN (Farabundo Marti National Liberation Front), backed by Cuba and the Soviet Union, waged a bitter, blood-soaked conflict. Over 75,000 people died, and according to most reports, the majority were innocent civilians. Thousands more simply disappeared, rumoured to be casualties of 'death squads' that would roam the countryside, killing and maiming anyone they met.

Helpless in the face of such lawlessness, another 500,000 Salvadorans fled the country – most of them to the US. In some cases entire families would escape; in others parents would leave their children to be raised by grandparents … or would send their children and stay behind themselves.

And it was in the Land of the Free that the seeds of El Salvador's current gang nightmare were sown.

Most of the refugees settled in the ghettos of Los Angeles. For penniless, often illegal, immigrants, life in the city was tough. Survival meant showing enough strength for others not to mess with you. And that meant finding a new kind of family.

Calle Dieciocho, or the 18th Street gang, was created as long ago as the late 1960s, and named after the Los Angeles street controlled by Central American immigrants to the city. By the 1980s and 90s, the sudden flood of Salvadorean refugees saw their membership snowball and they have now grown to become one of California's largest and most fragmented street gangs, with membership in the tens of thousands. Out of this, it is estimated that about 60 per cent of its members are illegal immigrants.

Thousands of Salvadoreans, arriving broke and terrified, having fled horrific bloodshed and left loved ones behind, flocked to the protection and sense of community offered by the 18th Street.

Initially, they didn't have much choice. For those who didn't join 18th Street, life in LA was a nightmare: they were alone, unprotected, vulnerable. And so they formed another gang: Mara Salvatrucha. Named after La Mara, a street in San Salvador, and the Salvatrucha guerillas who fought in El Salvador's bloody civil war, they learnt fast and hard. According to one of the founding MS members, interviewed for an American newspaper years later: 'In El Salvador's war we were taught to kill our own people, no matter if they were from your own blood. If your father was the enemy, you had to kill him. So the training we got during the war in our country served to make us one of the most violent gangs in the United States.'

Between them, 18th Street and MS were not only providing support and protection for the thousands of Salvadorean refugees arriving in Los Angeles; they were also becoming powerful, illegal, deadly enemies in the LA criminal underworld.

Too powerful, too illegal, too deadly.

In 1996 the Californian authorities acted. New anti-gang laws led to a crackdown on the Central American gangs – with deportation the prime sanction. Anyone who was not an American citizen, even if they were permanent residents, could, if sentenced to more than a year in prison, be deported – and even immigrants who had gained citizenship could be stripped of it and sent 'home' after serving their prison sentences.

The US government's attempts to clean up California had at its heart the systematic deportation of a whole newly trained criminal element. And now it's El Salvador's problem.

Tens of thousands were shipped out of LA. Many had lived most of their lives in America, some could not even speak Spanish, and most had little or no surviving family willing to take them in. So what were they to do?

They did the natural thing. They regrouped and re-created the LA gangs on home turf. El Salvador once again became a battleground: this time between MS and 18th Street, warring gangs made in America from Salvadorean refugees. They are a problem created out of civil war, honed in exile and now returned to exact a terrible price on the homeland.

The number of gang members on the streets grows daily. Every month 1,000 more are deported back to El Salvador from the United States.

The gangs are as sophisticated as they are uncompromising.

18th Street gang members are required to abide by a strict set of rules: they are forbidden from using crack cocaine and other hard drugs. Failure to obey the word of a gang leader, or to show proper respect to a fellow gang member, may result in an 18-second beating, or even execution for more serious offences.

The 18-second rule also applies to the initiation of new members: anyone wanting to become a part of 18th Street must endure a ritual beating by three or more members while the gang counts slowly to 18. Hitting back is not allowed – and if you can't take the punishment, you are banned from the gang. Not only that: your whole family are likewise shamed, and all of you declared fair game for gang members to do as they like to.

Both gangs insist on lifelong allegiance; and both demand that members prove that allegiance through tattoos. Indelible declarations of loyalty, they can range from a simple tag across the chest or upper arm to huge, elaborate memorials to fallen comrades covering their whole bodies – and even faces.

The tattoos are also, as we would see, the police force's best means of identifying El Salvador's most prolific criminals.

✵   ✵   ✵

We were about to go out on the streets with the Inteceptores, and Captain Umberto was laying it all down. The plan was simple: we would ride shotgun with him and a driver in the unmarked car – behind us would be the pick-up with the rest of his team. Everyone – including us – wore body armour; everyone – apart from us – carried automatic machine-guns with the safety catches permanently turned off. Each of them also wore a small sidearm.

We were headed into an area called Lourdes, just west of San Salvador, the capital. We were on a manhunt, trying to flush out a gang boss wanted for multiple murders.

As we all took our places and got going, Umberto explained the need for such heavy artillery.

'Our unit goes out with all necessary measures because the areas we cover are very high risk,' he told us. 'Sometimes we encounter gangs and have to confront them. And sometimes they carry more weapons than we do. And that is why we keep all our weapons ready all the time.' He hefted his machine-gun from his lap. 'This is a Galil rifle. The projectile it uses is practically the same as the M16. And the gun is a nine millimetre ...'

Outside, San Salvador was still sleepy in the morning sun. As we left the city centre and cruised through the surburban streets, there was none of the hustle and bustle of the capital ... low build-ings kept shutters closed, the traffic got scarcer, the only pedes-trians we saw slouched slowly along, going nowhere in particular, and taking their time about it too.

To be honest, it all looked pretty peaceful. With the air-con on full and the window open, Umberto was relaxed, leaning back in his seat, one elbow outside the car, the other arm resting on his machine-gun. He joked with the driver, recounting a story about one of the team who had recently had trouble with his wife and mistress ... We soaked up the view, taking in the bright washes of colour, the clear light, the dusty, mostly deserted streets. None of it said 'danger' to our minds. If anything, the images we were getting were more like a Michael Palin documentary – something gentle and heartwarming about the simple, poor, kindly folk of Central America ... not exactly the kind of footage we were after for a series about the world's toughest cops.

Appearances can be deceptive.

Umberto turned in his seat. 'We are now heading towards some of the more problematic areas,' he said. 'As well as looking for the suspect, we're going to see if we can find some of the other criminals operating. The mission is to intervene immediately – and proceed with arrests and searches. And if we can't find any …' he shrugged, 'then we'll keep patrolling in hope that we will find activities. We'll keep going until around 10 p.m.

'It's rare for us to remain at the base. We're out and about from 6 a.m. to midday and then from 2 till 11 p.m. But there are also occasions when we're around all night and until early morning.'

He grinned again, giving us a flash of that Clooney-esque charm. 'Who knows if this will be one of those days, eh?'

Out of the car window he pointed his hand at graffiti on all sides of buildings as we passed. To our eyes they just looked like the standard kind of tags you'd see anywhere in Britain or America – stylised names, harmless 'woz here' calling cards. Not so. These were markers of territory. And the same two letters kept coming up: MS. Mara Salvatrucha.

'As we can see here, these are graffiti belonging to the Mara Salvatrucha,' said Umberto, his voice slow, relaxed, just like someone narrating a tourist expedition, pointing out the sights from an open-topped bus. 'That's the rival to 18th Street. Round here they are in charge of committing a series of crimes – extortions, homicides, assault, killing people if they don't do as they are being told. That's what the MS gang members dedicate their time to. They've learnt to make money the easy way rather than to work for it. And they exploit the decent citizens living in the area. That's what they do. They've got used to committing crimes rather than looking for a job.

'Yesterday we arrested two members in one of these areas. You arrest them right away.'

Looking around to take in the graffiti – now we had noticed it, suddenly it was everywhere, covering every surface – we noticed something strange happening in the following pick-up truck. One of the Inteceptores in the back had pulled a balaclava from his pocket and was rolling it down over his face. These boys looked intimidating enough as it was – all black combats, black body armour and black automatic weapons – but the addition of a black balaclava made him look even more threatening.

Umberto saw us looking and explained. It seemed this particular officer was from Lourdes himself. He was the one who had fingered the murder suspects – they were practically his neighbours, people he sees every day. No one here knew he was a cop. If the gang members were to find out they'd been betrayed by someone in their neighbourhood then retribution would be swift and merciless – and they wouldn't be satisfied with teaching the officer himself a lesson. By leading the Inteceptores into his own backyard he was putting his whole family in danger. Little wonder he didn't want to show his face.

The mood had changed. Suddenly the streets didn't seem empty because of any laid-back, Hispanic *mañana* attitude; suddenly those few nonchalant figures we saw strolling around didn't seem so friendly. We were getting into gangland territory – and as part of a police unit, we were the enemy.

Moving slower now, the radio tuned to the 911 channel – 'just to see if there are any emergency calls, so we can intervene immediately' – our two-vehicle unit rolled through the streets and into a square.

Small trees lined the plaza, light dappling through the leaves on to a fountain. Water trickled from a statue; a group of small children played a game of tag around it. Another girl sat by herself on the fountain steps, texting or just playing with a mobile phone. She couldn't have been more than 10 or 11; she was barefoot and wore a simple flowery dress. Jet black hair fell forward over her face as she concentrated on the screen.

It was a breathtaking moment. Here, in the so-called heart of the MS gang territory, a picture-perfect image of innocence: small children playing tag around a fountain in the morning, another engrossed in her own world. We did wonder where she had found the mobile phone, but still it was a heartwarming scene.

'So,' said Umberto, leaning across the driver to point out of the window. 'All those kids that you see there are going to be future gang members. The ones behind us over there. Those three at the back – the little ones are the ones watching out for approaching police.'

We didn't think they had even noticed us.

The captain continued. 'That young girl sat over there to the right, she is one of those who sees a police car and gets on the phone. It doesn't look like it but she is part of the gang. As you can see, there she is on the phone. She doesn't have a tattoo but she takes note of every police car that gets into the area and passes the news on to her fellow gang members. She's texting them now, telling them we're here.'

Another illusion shattered. And, with it, any thoughts we might have had of catching the gang members by surprise. Flushing out the gang members in these winding alleyways is especially difficult. Tipped off by lookouts at the entrances to the neighbourhoods, the gangsters are able to simply disappear off the streets.

Suddenly the car lurched forward as the accelerator was floored, and the pick-up with the rest of the squad swerved around us and sped ahead as the man in the balaclava shouted directions. There was no time to lose. The man they were after, who lived around here, was wanted in relation to two recent homicides: his nickname on the streets was 'Sniper'.

A series of lurching turns and the next moment we were squealing to a stop. By the time we had got out of the car, Umberto's men had a suspect pinned against a wall, arms high, assuming the position. As the captain sauntered towards him, other officers scanned the surrounding low houses, weapons ready, fingers poised over triggers.

Casual as you like, Umberto pulled up the guy's vest. The tattoos said it all. This was the man we had come to find – and, more by luck than anything else, we'd stumbled across him just walking down the road.

Umberto asked him his name, even though he already knew it … and for the next 10 minutes the pair of them had the kind of pointless, back-and-forth conversation that only policemen and criminals ever engage in. The gang member offered up at least four false names; Umberto rejected them all, never once losing his cool, most of the time smiling, occasionally even laughing openly at the man for even bothering to try.

We got there in the end; a squad car was called, the suspect cuffed and taken away.

Umberto remained supremely relaxed, but all the time, at the back of the police squad, watching the road, was the officer in the balaclava. The suspect kept craning his head to see him: other officers kept jerking his attention away again. Meanwhile all the Inteceptores were constantly scanning the surrounding houses, and we couldn't help feeling the boy we had apprehended wasn't the only one taking an interest in our identities.

It seemed a lot of tension for one arrest – but Umberto reckons every collar's worth it. 'Catching a gang member is quite difficult at the moment because they have a good system of communication,' he said, as we got ready to move again. 'Including those children we saw, their own family members, even designated people in stores who advise them when the police are around.

'But residents of this community are people who have to deal with the circumstances they have been given in life, and that includes their children not being given a basic education. It's tough. Here, the MS gang charges everyone who enters the neighbourhood five dollars every time they enter. And there is always a gang leader responsible for working early with these children, for recruiting them when they're young, before they've had a chance to get out. Here, children at the age of 11 are already gang members.'

He shrugged, and motioned for the squad to ship out. 'But as of now there is one less gang leader on the streets here. And that's a good thing.'

✼ ✼ ✼

El Salvador may only be the size of Wales, and have a population smaller than Greater London's but it is also the most densely populated country in the Americas, has one of the highest murder rates in the world, and a crime occurs there every single minute.

Thirteen cars are hijacked or stolen every day – most end up used by the gangs for robberies and murders – and every 24 hours here sees 10 more Salvadoreans murdered. Cops don't fare much better: one police officer is killed every month.

No one is under any illusions as to the heart of the problem. Gangs have carved up this little country; and they've done it the easy way. With guns.

Weapons are everywhere here. One person in five carries a gun and, in a country where a hand grenade costs a dollar, life is – literally – cheap.

It's another bloody legacy of the civil war. If the 12-year conflict effectively created the Mara Salvatrucha and 18th Street gangs, it has also supplied them with a vast arsenal of deadly weapons. El Salvador is awash with arms left over from the war: every gang member is carrying – cops like the Inteceptores are no longer surprised to find kids even as young as 10 or 11 with a Glock stuffed down their shorts.

So much so that for many officers, it's not the older, hardened, veteran gang members they fear the most: instead it's the youngest, the new breed, the street kids with the most to prove and the least to lose.

Police reports estimate that 20,000 young people are currently gang members. The 18th Street gang is sometimes even referred to as the 'Children's Army' because of its active policy of recruiting children and young teenagers.

These are the kids Umberto was pointing out to us as we cruised into Lourdes – and these are the kids he's going to watch grow into thieves, drug dealers, murderers. It's a heartbreaker. Thinking back to the little girl with the mobile phone by the fountain, we couldn't help remembering the old phrase: the first casualty of war is innocence.

But if the civil war has created the worst of El Salvador's current problems, it has also left at least one positive legacy.

After the 1992 ceasefire, land was granted to the poor rural farmers and the control of public order was taken away from the army. A new police force was created, with the aim of finally ending the deadly conflict between rich and poor, left wing and right wing. Made up of both communist guerrillas and former republican officers, the National Civil Police force (or PNC) brought together Salvadoreans who had fought against one another during the war to fight crime side by side.

Today, 16 years after its creation, the PNC has 16,000 officers and, despite the dangers that the cops face on the streets of El Salvador, the National Academy sees 100 new recruits a month, all willing to lay their lives on the line for their country.

EL SALVADOR

The next generation of crime fighters are coming through: and just nine of them are good enough for Captain Umberto's Inteceptores.

Umberto is justifiably proud of his crack team.

'The unit was founded a year and three months ago,' he told us. 'Its mission is mainly to intervene in any crime situation. Any type of car hijack, any type of criminal activity, robbery, goods smuggling, gangs. At the moment we're mainly based around the capital, but as things progress and the unit grows larger the idea is that we'll stretch ourselves across the nation. That's mainly what we do.

'Much of our work is on the streets of San Salvador, listening into the 911 channel here in the capital to see if there are any emergency calls ... and if so we'll intervene immediately. We've achieved a lot in the last year and three months that we've been active. We've confiscated plenty of weapons, arrested gang members, confiscated stolen goods and a lot of other new activities.

'We've had a few challenges so far,' he said, and then, with his trademark smile and self-effacing shrug, he added: 'But nothing of huge importance. Remember that our job is quite risky, but we've always managed to keep on top of things ... but yes, there have been some confrontations between us involving gunfire and all that.

'But I would say that when a criminal is killed it just means there's one less useless person in our country. The best thing to do is – and, hey what do I know, right? – the best thing is to get rid of him. That's my point of view. Because that means that we've prevented him from causing further damage to others.'

Umberto himself has been in the force for 16 years, having signed up almost immediately after the ceasefire, one of the first men to pledge allegiance to the new PNC. Born and raised in the gang-ravaged colonias – the warren of ghettos controlled by the

MS and 18th Street – he knows these streets as well as any of the criminals he's hunting. He could have taken that route himself, he could have chosen the easy life of no work, fast cash, thrills and drugs and guns … but he made a harder decision. He chose to try to help his country.

We wanted to know why. Umberto thought about that for a while, staring out of the car window as the streets zipped by, eyes glittering under his low cap. His eventual answer was as simple as it was impressive.

'Because I've never been scared of anything,' he said.

✳   ✳   ✳

Our next stop with Umberto was Quezaltepeque. A few miles north of San Salvador, it's home to one of the country's largest prisons and is a renowned Mara Salvatrucha stronghold. El Salvador has a prison capacity of 7,500, which sounds a pitiful amount – until you recall that the population is less than seven million.

Still, it's nowhere near enough. It's estimated there are nearly 19,000 criminals locked up, and with prisons overflowing the little space they do have needs to be reserved for the gang leaders. So what happens? Prisons become recruitment stations, training camps, hothouses for the gangs. Those rare criminals who might enter Quezaltepeque prison without MS tattoos won't leave that way – unless it's in a bodybag.

On the way north, we read Umberto a cutting we'd found amongst the research into El Salvador's gang culture. One of the Mara Salvatrucha's proudest achievements, it said, was when gang members broke into the country's parliament buildings and left a dismembered corpse with a note for the president promising: '… more people will die … the next victims will be police and journalists.'

Umberto laughed. He liked that one, he said. Police and journalists. We were a car full of police and journalists, after all. As if he wasn't hated enough by the gangs as it was, he laughed, now the presence of a British documentary crew made him even more of a target. He seemed to think it was hilarious.

I've known men – on the pitch and off – who welcome a challenge like that, who relish the thought of taking someone's personal hatred and turning it to their advantage ... but not like this. Not laughing off death threats.

We asked him to tell us, if he never got scared, what his family thought about the daily dangers? One dead cop a month isn't the kind of statistic to inspire confidence in the police as a career choice.

'Well, in the beginning my family didn't want me to be part of the police force,' he admitted. 'They were scared because we have lost quite a few officers to crime in the past. The family always gets worried watching the news and reading the papers. So they were telling me not to join ... but I chose to do it and, thank God, here we are.

'One of my brothers used to be in the police force but I'm not sure about what happened to him. He had some problems and he emigrated to the US. He's now been in America for 12 years and he is happy there, so ...' he shrugged. 'Good for him, I guess. But I like it here in the force and the truth is that I never wanted to leave my country. I'm happy to stay here in the PNC. I prefer to stay here, in spite of the fact we have to suffer calamities and the salary is no good. As for my family – well, they still ask me to be careful out there, but they've learnt to accept it.'

Umberto's family situation isn't totally straightforward. Like so many other dedicated cops, his commitment to the job has cost him his home life.

'I was married for six years,' he told us, 'and during that time I had problems with my wife. Now I'm divorced and I haven't married again, I'm single, with two children. They are with her family, they stay with my ex-wife's mum. I have one son of 12 and a daughter of six years.

'My son – sometimes when I speak with him by phone, or when I pick him up for a weekend, he says to me that he wants to be policeman when he grows up … but at the same time he says, and imagine this, he is only 12 years old, he says he doesn't like it because of what he sees on TV. Sometimes he calls me and he says that he has just seen something on TV, some injured policemen … and all I can tell him is that he has not to be worried. All I can say is "I will tell you whatever happens".'

Umberto wouldn't tell us if he would like to see his son follow him into the PNC. To his way of thinking, it's something you can only choose for yourself – and not the kind of job you can do unless you're 100 per cent committed to the cause.

Umberto himself demands that dedication from his Inteceptores. Their long days on the streets are made longer by a rigorous training regime: up at 4.30 a.m. and in the gym, followed by a six-kilometre run before breakfast. And then a full day on the front line in the war against gangs.

He may seem a pretty laid-back guy, but Umberto doesn't mess around professionally: and if you can't handle the pace, you're no good to him. He wants the Inteceptores to be the best of the best, the unit that's going to show just how the blood-soaked streets of this gang-infested country can be cleaned up.

'What makes me motivated?' he asks back, in response to our question. 'It's the action. Always. When we are in a high-risk situation, when we catch a dangerous criminal. That's what motivates me. I love it. Because … it's something …' he struggled to find the right words, waving his arms around the car. 'It's something … it's not a normal job. When we catch a criminal and we realise that he is guilty of a lot of homicides, you feel like … your morale get high, you know? That's what I like the best. The action. Doing the right thing.'

✿ ✿ ✿

The rest of the day was taken up in mop-ups and rapid response – cruising the colonias, looking for action, shaking down suspected gang members, raiding known gang hangouts. As the sleepy morning turned into a baking afternoon, the radios were tuned to the 911 channel, and Umberto and his men remained in a constant state of readiness, primed to drop everything and fly across town if needed.

It was exhausting keeping up with them … but you wouldn't think it to see Umberto himself. Never anything but relaxed, he took it all in his stride, from racing through twisting alleys and jammed streets to pinning gang members against a wall and frisking them for weapons.

In Quezaltepeque we raided a pool hall: word had come through that it was being used as a Mara Salvatrucha base. Once again, because of the possibility that every kid we passed in the neighbourhood could be alerting the gang bosses that we were in the area, speed was the key. The car and pick-up screamed through the alleyways, skidding to a stop outside a one-storey shack – the pool hall was little more than four whitewashed walls and a bit of corrugated iron for a roof. We were still moving when the team jumped out and burst through the doors, machine-guns first.

As we watched through the window of the squad car, three boys were led out and frisked down – they couldn't have been more than 17 or 18. Stripped to the waist, the now familiar black ink stood out on their skin: they had tattoos all right, but a quick scan by Umberto confirmed they weren't gang markers.

The boys weren't carrying either – apart from one knife, a thin, nasty-looking thing hidden down one of their socks. Umberto confiscated it and let them get back to their game.

'We searched the citizens inside this pool hall, because criminals often hide in these places,' he explained, once the squad were back and moving again. 'You have to be careful because you don't know the kind of people you could find. Thank God in there everything was under control. We only found one knife, which we confiscated.'

Next stop was Soyapango, a poor, gritty colonia on the east side of San Salvador, and a former leftist guerrilla stronghold. This area is at the centre of a fierce turf war between the two gangs over control of the lucrative protection rackets bleeding local businesses. It's a war fought street to street, building to building: in Soyapango, the MS and the 18th Street gangs live within yards of each other.

'Soyapango is an area full of conflicts,' Umberto warned us as we slowed to a cruise, his eyes scanning the streets, staring down the alleyways as we rolled past them. 'There are gang members here, both MS and 18th Street. They commit a series of crimes. Murders, extortions, robbery, illegal weapons. Anything you can think of. Any time during the day and night there are murders in these areas.'

Remembering his precise assessment of our chances of survival without him in Lourdes, we couldn't resist asking Umberto for his view on just how likely it is to see a murder here on the average day.

He turned and gave us a slow smile: if he knew we were making fun of him, he was cool with it. 'I'd say almost 75 per cent chance of murder today,' he said. 'We're used to seeing it. Are you?'

Suddenly there was a burst of siren from the pick-up and Umberto snapped back to attention. Two men slouched along the road in front of us: within seconds we were all over them.

Sure enough, the tattoos confirmed it: 18th Street. They were searched, questioned, bundled into the back of the pick-up ready to go to the station. No further evidence was needed: just being in a gang gave the Inteceptores grounds for arrest.

As they were unloaded again at the nearest station, we managed to get a word with them. Again, barely out of their teens, they looked more scared than dangerous, despite the tattoos. We wanted to know if they enjoyed being part of the 18th Street. 'To start with, yes,' said one, 'but later on, it's not fun any more. The other gang have already killed two of my brothers.'

We couldn't help wondering just how young he was when he was recruited – and what crimes he had committed for the cause.

As soon as they had been deposited, the squad were back on the road. This was how it went some days, Umberto explained. Some days had more action then others.

We were taking a well-earned break in Burger King. 'In America the cops eat doughnuts,' one of the Inteceptores joked with us. 'In El Salvador we eat meat. Like real men – you tell them that when you get home: El Salvador cops eat only beef!' The rest of the squad cracked up, but Umberto himself leant in with a serious look on his face.

'The boys laugh,' he told our crew, 'but for me it hasn't been the most successful day.' He gave his now familiar shrug. 'At least we've had a few arrests. We've prevented some criminal activity. We had one MS arrest in Lourdes. And we also had two other 18th Street arrests here in Soyapango. I hope that the crime will start going down slowly as we're always on the alert and should be able to make things better day by day. Reducing the violence is not a thing that we can accomplish overnight. It's not as simple as that.'

But if Umberto had remained calm, laid-back and unflappable throughout the day, everything was about to change. And his casual, half-joking assessment of the murder risk in Soyapango was about to be proved, suddenly, horribly real.

✻　　✻　　✻

We had just left our burgers and were getting back into the cars when a commotion behind and above us changed everything. From where we were, steps led up a steep bank to a road on a higher level – and we looked up to see six or seven figures up there, waving frantically, shouting for help.

'Murder! Murder! *Asesinato!*'

Umberto didn't waste any time. The team sprang into action – one man into each of the vehicles, covering both routes up to the bank, the rest legging it up the steps, guns held ready, eyes everywhere.

Umberto led the charge. The scene at the top was horrific.

A café – barely even a café, just a collection of tables and chairs with a bar – empty, all the customers at one end. Some of them screaming, some crying, some just staring. At the other end, a mess of chairs, an upturned table. A spilt coffee. A sandwich on the floor. And two human bodies.

One lay on his back under a table, his legs still on the seat. His face was a mess of blood and shattered bone; the back of his head lay in a puddle of pooling red liquid. The other had been thrown clear of the café itself: he lay shirtless, sprawled on the edge of the bank. Angry scarlet bullet wounds marked his chest and leg. Both were completely still.

Just a few minutes before, both men had been enjoying a drink: now both were dead.

We stared, hypnotised by the stark, simple brutality of it. Gunshot wounds really do look like they do in the movies; blood really does splatter everywhere when a man's been shot point blank in the face. And already the flies were moving in. We felt sick: but at the same time we couldn't turn our eyes away from the carnage.

Umberto, meanwhile, moved through the murder scene quickly, carefully, taking it all in, stepping from one body to the other, speaking fast and calmly into his radio. 'We've got two dead bodies here that were shot five to ten minutes ago,' he said, never pausing as he walked around the men, assessing the angles, trying to work out from their positions just where and how they had been shot. 'Two unknown persons came and killed them.' He named the café and gave instructions to the Crime Scene Investigator Unit and the ambulances. 'Get them to come in via the main road and we'll be waiting for them here,' he finished, and immediately turned to the worried-looking witnesses.

It was a frustrating moment. Unable to leave the scene until backup arrived, Umberto knew nevertheless that the gang members who committed the crime must still be nearby. He was itching to get after them, chase them down ... but old-fashioned police work took precedence over adrenaline and instinct.

As the Inteceptores started grilling the bystanders, Umberto moved between them, listening intently, but also scanning all their faces, subtly checking their clothes, bare arms, bare legs. With a jolt we realised he was looking for signs of gang membership. The shooting was so recent, the gunmen could still be amongst this crowd.

Eventually, with a wail of sirens, backup arrived. As the medics ran in, Umberto pointed them towards the murder scene. 'They are already dead. They are both dead but they're over there. They were dead when we got here,' he said, and after a quick debrief with the CSI team, he nodded at his Inteceptores and we prepared to move out.

'I think it's quite clear that these deaths were caused by MS gang members,' he told us, as we sprinted for the cars. 'This is where the MS gang tend to operate. According to those witnesses who would tell us anything at all, the killers are supposedly hiding here in the alleyways.

'This is the problem that we have here, no one sees anything. I asked the owner of the place what happened and guess what? She didn't see anything.' He gave a short, hollow laugh and shook his head. 'And this only just happened.

'Anyway. Let's see what we can do now. We'll drive off quickly to see if we can find any traces of them.'

Umberto was fired up again, leaning round his seat to keep us up to date. 'So what we did learn is that one of the subjects is wearing a yellow shirt, and the other a white one,' he said. 'They've been seen running away through the alleyways. This area is very colourful and full of MS gang members. The criminals that committed this must be somewhere around here in one of the alleys ...'

We careered through the narrow, twisting streets, sirens off, accelerating in short bursts and slowing again every time we caught a glimpse of a likely candidate. The radio jabbered constantly with updates, more info on the victims, the killers. For over an hour we covered every inch of the colonia ... and for over an hour we got nothing. The murderers had split.

Uncooperative witnesses, the delay caused by waiting for backup, the warren of alleyways that make up the colonia itself ... any one of these things might have meant the difference between catching the killers and returning to base empty-handed.

'If we had got here a bit earlier, we would have had them,' muttered Umberto to himself, pulling his cap down lower over eyes that glittered with fierce frustration.

He turned to us, still in the back of the car. 'So the latest thinking is that apparently the killers got a taxi out of the area.' He frowned. 'So it doesn't seem we're going to pick them up today.'

We asked if there were any further leads on why the shooting took place. Were the victims gang members too?

He shook his head. 'The reason for these deaths, according to how I've analysed it as a policeman, is that this was nothing more than a robbery. It could be that the deaths were caused because of an issue over rent – the famous 'rent' that they forcibly charge people to come into the area. Maybe they refused to give it to them and so those guys were waiting for them. Simple as that: they ask you for a certain amount of dollars … and if you don't give it to them, they kill you.

'Here in our country, your days are practically numbered. If you're not alert, if you're not attentive … in seconds you can lose your life. Just like those two citizens lost their lives sitting there drinking coffee – they were just ordinary workers from the nearby factory. In this area … in all the areas we've been in today, murders happen all the time. And the big problem, and what we've seen with the two murders this afternoon, is that citizens don't want to co-operate. They don't say, "Listen he went that way", out of fear that they're going to get killed, because in these areas, if you divulge information as a witness, then the next day, you're getting it yourself.

'In El Salvador, the value of life is that cheap.'

BADLANDS: BORDER PATROL WITH JESSE JIMENEZ

Laredo, Texas. By far the smallest city we would visit in America, it's also home to one of the biggest crime problems facing the entire United States. This desert town on the banks of the Rio Grande is a key point for trade between the US and Mexico – and that's where the trouble starts.

Across the river lies Nuevo Laredo. Four bridges link the cities – and every day thousands of trucks cross the border. Not all of them are legit. They call this place smuggler's paradise: people, drugs, guns – all of them are shipped over the river, every day, and in huge numbers. Billions of criminal dollars, moved through this city the size of Leicester, headed for all parts of the US – and all controlled by ruthless criminal gangs and Mexican cartels who don't think twice about killing anyone who gets in their way.

Up against them are officers like Jesse Jimenez from the Sheriff's Department. He spends his shifts patrolling the highways, raiding stash houses, picking up illegal immigrants and looking for contraband. It's a massive task, a relentless slog, a never-ending battle against over-whelming odds. But Jesse does it anyway. He does it because he believes that every arrest, every bust, every confiscated shipment makes a difference.

His enthusiasm for the fight was infectious. And as we found out, his job wasn't just about the action, the adrenaline, the glory: Jesse was part of a new way of policing. Believe it or not, he actually cared. It was a privilege to ride with him.

✧   ✧   ✧

IT WAS ON OUR LAST AFTERNOON in Laredo when we got the call we'd been hoping for. The mobile read 'number withheld', but we answered on the first ring anyway.

Sure enough, it was our man. His clear, precise voice – well-brought-up Texan American with just a lilt of street Hispanic to it – was unmistakable.

'Vinnie? It's Jesse. Are you still in town? We've got something for you. Something big.'

We were moving before the conversation even ended. Jesse Jimenez had come through for us: we knew he would. We'd finally get to see just what the cops in this town are really chasing … something more worthwhile than immigrants and desperate border crossings.

Something with a street value running into millions, he said. He sounded pretty pleased with himself. He had every right to.

We chucked everything into the car and promised him we'd be there as fast as the speed limits in this state allowed.

* * *

The first thing we learnt about Officer Jesus Jimenez of the Sheriff's Department was not to call him Jesus. 'It's Jesse, man,' he said with a big smile of the whitest teeth we'd ever seen. 'Nobody calls me Jesus except my mom.'

Jesse it was then. I didn't have the heart to tell him what Jesse means to most Englishmen … and I was a little bit gutted I couldn't explain the old 'Jesus Saves – but so does Peter Shilton' joke, but still. He probably wouldn't have the faintest idea who Shilts was anyway.

And the bottom line was this. We were in the Wild West – and we were riding with the sheriff's man. Come on – it's every boy's dream come true, right?

LAREDO

Laredo really is the Wild West. This has always been bandit country, and even if it's no longer about cowboys and injuns, these days it's America's front line in a different, though no less bloody, war. The city lies on the Rio Grande in southern Texas – Mexico's just a stone's throw across the water. Crime gangs and international smuggling cartels make billions from this border, and keep their business lucrative through a ruthless blend of fear and bloody violence.

The Rio Grande runs the length of US–Mexico border for about 750 miles. Everything that's smuggled into Texas has to come across this river. This is the international dividing line.

In the 1960s Laredo was the poorest city in America, and although it's now the second-fastest growing city, the average wage is still only £150 a week. But make no mistake: there's money here all right. Pots of money. And a whole lot of it stinks to high heaven.

Laredo is an important centre for legitimate trade – it is after all an international border city with checkpoints on each of its four bridges. On both sides of the border the multi-lane highways leading to those entry points are backed up for miles with lines of huge trucks. Millionaires are created from the legal import/export business here … but it's the illegal trade that makes billions.

Over 10,000 cargo trucks pass through Laredo every day on their way to Interstate 35 and cities throughout the US. They are matched by another 10,000 cars, vans, 4x4s … which adds up to over 20,000 vehicle crossings a day. At such high volumes, it is impossible for US customs to stop, search and process every vehicle. This border crossing is a smuggler's dream.

Every bridge across the Rio Grande has its checkpoints, but it's not enough. The cartels smuggle drugs and people into the USA and don't think twice about killing to protect their profit. It's reckoned that around $10 million worth of drugs cross over the four bridges into Laredo every day: in just one weekend last year, the cops here seized $11 million worth of cocaine and three tonnes of marijuana.

And then there are the illegal immigrants. Some come over in small, desperate groups of twos and threes, or as families, chancing it in cars or boats, even swimming; the rest are ferried like cattle as 'customers' of the cartels, who charge them a small fortune for passage across the border and the promise of a new life in America.

It's not one-way traffic, however. Demand is almost as high for exports to Mexico as it is for imports to Laredo ... or rather, for one export in particular. In Texas, anyone can buy a gun, but in Mexico it's against the law. This makes the situation all the more efficient for the cartels: drugs and people are smuggled one way over the river; illegal firearms are transported back the other way.

Laredo's sister city, Nuevo Laredo, lies directly across the border. It is a lawless, violent place, all but ruled by the cartels and with a higher murder rate than LA, Chicago and New York. The deadly crime wave is so out of control there that the Mexican government has even had to call in the army to protect its people.

As murder rates in Nuevo Laredo sky-rocketed, in 2005 Mexico's President Vicente Fox launched 'Operation Safe Mexico', dispatching 1,500 soldiers to Nuevo Laredo and other northern cities where the cartels had taken control.

In Nuevo Laredo alone, 140 local police officers were fired, suspected of corruption. Within a year another 57 cops were sacked and, in early 2006, Nuevo Laredo's police chief, Omar

Pimentel, resigned after only eight months in charge. Gunmen had killed his predecessor just seven hours into the job.

The US cops do not want that situation in their city. Keeping the anarchy on the other side of the river is a constant battle and a massive task for a small force. It calls for complete dedication.

We were here to experience that dedication for ourselves – and to find out what it takes to be the sheriff in this town. And that meant saddling up with a man called Jesus.

And that's not the kind of thing you find yourself saying every day.

❉   ❉   ❉

We met Jesse outside the station as he prepared for a night shift. He looked in his late twenties, maybe 30 at a push, and clearly kept himself in good shape. He didn't have the bulk and muscle of some of the other cops we'd met – his physique was more athletic, more controlled. He carried himself easily, fluidly, like a runner or a martial artist. He also – and it was a bit strange to think this, but once it was there we couldn't get it out of our heads – looked a little bit like Tom Cruise in *A Few Good Men*. The straight white teeth did it, for sure, as well as the military-style crew cut and the clean-shaven skin … but he also had that open, friendly, well-mannered all-American thing going on. He called me Vinnie from the off, and insisted we call him Jesse.

As we went through the now familiar routine of strapping on the bullet-proof vests he also let us into a secret. He was up for promotion. All being well this would be one of his final patrols on the highways of Laredo – he was in contention for a position as an investigator with the Narcs. That's narcotics to you and me.

No time for congratulations yet, though. Tonight there was business to be done. Outlaws were on the road.

As we pulled out of the city and headed north on Route 83, the urban sprawl gradually gave way to smaller houses and run-down, semi-rural areas, before finally petering out altogether. And after that? Desert. Nothing but desert, as far as the eye could see. A flat, featureless, dusty wasteland with only this highway running straight as a bullet through the middle of it.

Route 83 cuts almost due north, parallel with the Mexican border, for 150 miles – headed towards Dallas and, from there, all parts of the US. It is an infamous smuggling highway.

We eventually pulled over by the side of the road ... and waited. Jesse kept an ear on the radio and both eyes on every vehicle that passed. We couldn't work out what he was looking for. Our only guess was that it wasn't anything in particular. He was working on instinct.

It was gone 9 p.m. and still nearly 100 degrees outside. Despite the air-con it felt like we were cooking in Jesse's car, wrapped up in the bullet-proofs, boiling from the inside out.

But the temperature was nothing, of course, compared to how hot it gets during the day. And that, as well as the darkness, made this prime time for the smugglers. Bodies packed in vehicles without air-conditioning, without drinking water, sometimes without even much air to breathe, have a nasty habit of dying when you try to transport them through the heat of the desert afternoon. Better wait till the sun goes down.

The radio was alive with noise – Jesse listened intently for a while and then shook his head. 'Right now they're calling false alarms in,' he said. 'What the smugglers do, they make prank calls so we get dispatched out of the area, so we all go somewhere and they can move their people and their narcotics out. That's what they're doing right now. They've just called in a fire and one of our units went out to respond to it and guess what? There was no fire.'

Another couple of cars zoomed by and Jesse leaned forward in his seat, staring after them intently. We couldn't stand it any more: he had to be looking for something. We asked him what.

He grinned. 'I guess it's a combination of everything. You look at the driver, you look at the car – sometimes the car doesn't even fit the person driving it, if you know what I mean. Sometimes you can just see that car doesn't even belong to that person. Also I'm trying to see what they're doing in the car. Whenever they see a patrol unit like this one they start talking into their radio. That's how they communicate with each other. They may be scouts that come on to the highway and scout for any patrol units. And then say "Come out, it's clear".'

But he still reckoned it was worth our while sitting here, even if we had been spotted. 'Sure,' he said, 'they get brave because they have got to move them out some time. One trick they try is to move out three vehicles at a time. That way they know if one of them falls maybe one of the others will get through. It's a risk they are willing to take.

'They might get away once, even twice. But they will get caught.' He smiled again. 'Vinnie, these guys will try anything to try and smuggle through, and they always end up getting caught. Sooner or later they will end up getting caught.

'They try everything. Anything. But we pick up on their trends. You know we have cameras, right? Whenever you think that no one is watching, there is actually people monitoring. We've got cameras, we've got sensors, so if a group is moving through the sensors they are going to get picked up. They will get caught.'

But still they come. Why? The answer's simple. And despite Jesse's confidence in the system, the fact is the Laredo cops are simply overwhelmed by the sheer numbers they're up against.

'These guys are making millions of dollars, billions,' he said. 'Millions are being made everyday. We're just scratching the surface. Someone did statistics and we are getting, like, five per cent of what's coming.'

Finally, we made a move. A couple of cars came past that Jesse didn't like the look of: he radioed another officer further up the road, who pulled them over. Moments later we were powering north to join them.

When we got there, Jesse's colleagues from the Sheriff's Department were already questioning the occupants of one of the cars. Two girls stood in the scrub by the side of the road, arms folded, eyes downcast.

Jesse nodded. 'This was the car,' he said. 'This one felt wrong.'

We hung back as he joined the other officers, speaking first to one girl, then the other, before filling us in. 'This is something that we try to do, you know, we try and get their story and try to see what the other party says. And then, when they got conflicting stories, usually that's an indicator that something is going on illegally.'

These girls had conflicting stories. Their ID was Mexican, they had no resident cards or paperwork to be in the US legally. It looked like they were another couple of runners making a dash for a better life. That they had got this far must have made it all the more heartbreaking for them. Jesse's colleagues led them away in tears.

'They're gonna be taken into custody by border patrol right now,' he explained. 'The driver was legal but the two passengers weren't. But they all say she wasn't doing it for profit. The driver will probably be facing some time.'

And then? All the Laredo cops can do is take them back over the river. 'Our responsibility is just to take them to the border. Just take them back to Mexico. A lot of times as soon as you throw them back over there, they just come back again.'

It was a result, I guess. It didn't exactly feel heroic, though – a couple of sad-faced Mexican girls pulled over in the desert and hauled back across the river. Jesse seemed like a great guy – but we weren't here to see him pick off runaways. We wanted a proper bust. There are billions being made here: we wanted to see a slice of it.

* * *

Back in the city we hooked up with Investigator Joe Baeza, a 10-year veteran of the force. He reckoned he could get us to shadow the SWAT unit on a raid: they were moving on the property of a suspected cartel kingpin – and we had a front row seat if we wanted it.

We didn't have to think too long before answering.

Joe himself was older than Jesse – with his thinning hair, aviator shades and slow, measured way of talking, he gave the impression of a cop who was no longer surprised by anything the job threw at him. And he was pretty no-nonsense in his assessment of what it is they do here too. If Jesse is part of the clean-cut, efficient new generation, Joe's old school.

'We will do whatever it takes to maintain stability and safety in our community and also for the rest of the United States,' he told us as he drove us to the SWAT briefing. 'The buck definitely stops here.

'The cartels, the drug pushers, they all use this great veil, this great forest of truck traffic to hide their narcotics going into the United States. If we rest, they win and people's lives are changed because of it. And the cost at times is the ultimate sacrifice.'

The briefing was short and to the point. The Special Weapons and Tactics Unit had a search warrant for the family home of a jailed Pistolero gang member. The Pistoleros control the gun smuggling in Laredo. Recently the police locked up a leader of the gang, one Roy Mendoza.

They now had a warrant to search his family home for drugs and weapons. Mendoza's son was thought to be living there, although he had no previous convictions. They were expecting to find firearms there – and they were prepared for some of those weapons to be used.

The plan was simple. The team were going for what they call a 'hard entry' – striking fast and without warning. The lead vehicle, an armoured personnel carrier known as a Bear Cat – just like we'd seen in New Orleans – was going to literally tear the gates down, and the unit would pour in through the resulting breech. All were to be fully armed and armoured: AR15s, M16s, Colt 9mm submachine-guns as standard. Vests, balaclavas and helmets – even though it was over 110 degrees. These boys weren't messing around.

The mood was pumped, edgy, taut with adrenaline. Everyone was psyching themselves up for the hit, each going through his own private little ritual. Some joked, slapping each other's backs and laughing hard; others were concentrating on their equipment, focusing their minds through the careful checking and rechecking of every piece of their gear.

By the time we all piled into the stifling Bear Cat, I was reminded of the atmosphere just before a massive football game.

It was the closest I'd come to feeling that again – everyone was buzzing, everyone wound up and hyped for it … only, of course, about a million times more intense than I'd ever felt in a dressing-room. It wasn't a case of these boys putting it all on the line for 90 minutes against Man United: they were getting ready to risk their lives. This was the real thing.

The tension built as we drove … until the order finally came. Showtime.

The Bear Cat pulled up outside a grand, sprawling place – a mansion, in fact. All the properties in this street were set well back from the road; they all had big iron gates and railings. There was money here.

The troop all jumped out of the transport at once, every gun held ready, every finger poised. Some of them shouted as they went and I couldn't help myself: 'GO ON BOYS!' I yelled, 'GO ON!' I was shaking with adrenaline – if someone had given me a rifle I swear I'd have stormed the place with them.

A line was thrown around the gates and reattached to the Bear Cat. One wheel-spinning reverse later and they lay wrenched and twisted on the ground. As the SWAT team moved in there was suddenly a commotion down the road. A car was backing up the street – then it crashed into another vehicle and the driver took off on foot.

Three officers legged it after him, running full-pelt despite their bulky armour and the burning heat. Almost before he had a chance to put his hands up and surrender they were on top of him. It was our man: Mendoza Junior. He was maybe 30 years old, chubby, with a shaved head and a cockiness about him, despite the fact that we'd just smashed into his family home.

By the time they had cuffed and cautioned him and hauled him back up to the house ready to witness whatever the team would bring out of it, Mendoza had regained all his cool. He even managed to laugh at the officers as they told him they were about to search the property for contraband.

Cocky little sod.

Finally, the house was declared safe by the SWAT boys and we followed the rest of the cops in to see what we could find.

If the outside reeked of money, the inside was straight out of the Mafia Man's Guide to Home Improvement. Polished glass, enormous mirrors, black and white leather furniture ... and an enormous marble bar on which was inlaid, in huge letters: 'MENDOZA'. Classy.

The best touch of all, however, had to be the painting above the fireplace. Al Pacino in *Scarface*, machine-gun in hand, in all his bloodied, insane 'Say hello to my l'il friend' glory – six foot by four foot, dominating the room.

'Hey, Vinnie,' called one of the cops. 'The quintessential poster for every bad guy's house, right?'

I've got the same poster in my office.

Laughs aside, there wasn't too much else going on. The team turned the place upside down, they got the dogs in, they even stripped Mendoza himself down to make sure he wasn't hiding anything in his pants ... and they got nada.

It seemed ridiculous. Mendoza was totally upfront about the fact he wasn't working, his dad was inside as one of the top men in the Pistoleros, Laredo's biggest gun-smuggling gang, this house was clearly worth millions – it was unbelievable that there should be nothing here we could pin on him.

One of the cops showed us a room that helped explain it a little. A bank of TV monitors showed views from CCTV cameras monitoring the outside of the property. Those, combined with a network of lookouts ready to call in about any potential raids headed this way, almost certainly meant that Mendoza had warning that we were coming and enough time to lose anything incriminating.

Outside, he was still laughing about it.

'The only shit that I'm going to say,' he said to us, grinning, 'is that I already knew everything, that they were coming. It's because they talk too much. They say we're gonna hit this ... they talk too much to their girlfriends, you see? They talk too much to their girlfriends, the girlfriends goes and tells their daughters, the daughters goes and tells me. They talk too much shit – so that's how everybody knows.'

Without anything else to go on, the cops could only charge him with resisting arrest – he would be released before nightfall.

It was a real downer. Half an hour earlier we'd been shaking with adrenaline, pumped up for a big score – and now, after the storm had settled and everything had calmed down, we were left with nothing.

He knew we were coming. In the end he was enjoying it all because he felt like he won the day. But the truth is, after an operation like that, you don't win the day. Because the Laredo cops were not about to leave it like that. It might take a little more time, it might take another operation, or two operations, or three or four ... but they will nail him eventually.

As one of the boys said on the way back to the station, Mr Mendoza Junior is going to have to be on his toes 24/7 from now on if he doesn't want to join his dad in the slammer.

✵　　✵　　✵

We were up for it now, itching for action. And that meant getting back on the road with Jesse Jimenez.

It was sunset when he picked us up, the start of another shift. But this time, instead of heading north on Route 83, we looked south. The sky was all pinks and oranges as we pulled into a car park outside a mall and prepared to hook up with Jesse's colleagues from the Sheriff's Department.

He looked as fresh, clean-cut and well-pressed as he had the last time we saw him. By the end of the night that would change. A tip had come in about an address suspected of being used as a safe house for drugs and illegal immigrants, and the sheriff's men were getting ready to roll.

'This is the southern part of Laredo right here,' he explained. 'It's not too violent, a pretty quiet neighbourhood … We're about to meet up at a restaurant called Whataburger and we'll try and get some more information on the target house. And see what we expect to find.'

The cops greeted Jesse with handshakes and back-slaps and quickly filled us in on the situation. Their CI – or confidential informant – had made contact with the stash house: now it was a case of just hanging around for the green light to go.

As we waited, the skies grew dark. The restaurant car park filled up – with families in cars, couples, even a few truckers, easing their rigs into the specially designated area for lorries, looking for a bite to eat before hitting the interstate towards Dallas. We couldn't help eyeing those trucks, wondering exactly what their cargo might be.

Finally, a mobile buzzed. The raid was confirmed. Two suspects had been spotted at the target house. It was our cue, and within minutes the nine officers and five cars were out of Whataburger and speeding towards the stash house. We were with Jesse in the front car.

Three or four corners later and it was sirens and headlights off. Jesse idled at a junction, staring intently left, right, left again. The target house was yards away, just across the road.

We couldn't understand the delay. What was he looking at?

'This is a residential area,' he said, always the community-minded, all-American cop. 'I don't want to just rush in here, there might be kids outside riding their bikes and I don't want them crossing the street and … you know there might be an accident …'

It was a new one on us. A cop delaying a raid to check for children crossing the road? The funny thing was, when he put it like that, we couldn't really argue with him. Even with a target in sight, Jesse was thinking of the bigger picture: his job is, after all, to protect the citizens of this town. Bottom line. Taking out bad guys is one part of it – making sure there are no innocents caught up in the crossfire is another.

Satisfied all was safe, he flashed his lights to the following units and eased us round the corner. 'OK,' he said, grinning. 'Dismount. Let's go.'

Our doors were barely open when a shout came out from one of the other cops. 'They're running! They're running!'

The doors to the target house had burst open and the two suspects had taken off, streaking down the street, jumping over fences and disappearing. Jesse was right after them, automatic rifle in hand, the torch mounted to the barrel jerking crazily back and forth as he ran.

Over one fence, through a garden, over another, across someone's yard … the runners were headed dead west, straight towards the river. The Mexican border was just two miles away and meant safety if they could reach it.

Jesse wasn't about to let that happen.

Suddenly he stopped. We were in a backstreet now, trailers on one side, a chainlink fence on the other. Ahead we could hear other cops shouting as they ran. Jesse stayed absolutely still, his gun pointed at the floor next to a trailer, the torch lighting up a circle of dirt, sand and fag butts. There was a moment of total calm and then … he dropped to his knees, shone the light underneath the trailer and with his spare hand hauled out a terrified-looking Mexican kid.

'We got one!' he shouted and slapped the cuffs on, and then, as back-up arrived, took off again.

By this time Jesse's shirt was soaked wet through with sweat, but he kept the pace up for another three blocks or so, sweeping his beam as he ran, checking every potential hiding-place he passed. No good. Eventually he had to concede defeat, and we jogged back to the car – just in time to see the suspect we had caught being driven away. One look at his wide-eyed, confused face told us he was no part of any drugs cartel. These boys were illegals, nothing more, nothing less. They were most likely hiding out at the house before trying to make their way further into Texas.

It didn't change what had happened, though. When Jesse ran them down, he didn't know if they were just desperate kids from over the border or seasoned, ruthless gangsters ready to kill to protect their stash.

'You don't know if he's behind a wall waiting for you with a gun in hand,' he confirmed, hands on his hips and blowing hard. His face shone with sweat and his shirt was soaked. 'You know, they could be ready to shoot at you when you come around the corner, you have to keep your weapon raised.

'You don't know really who you're running after. You can be running after one of the drug cartels, or one of the gang members, or a hitman or somebody that just committed murder. You just never, never know who you're running after, so you gotta be prepared for anything. It just comes natural, I think, with the train-ing – after doing it so many times your training kicks in and you're on automatic mode and you really don't have much time to think about consequences or anything. You just react to training and hopefully everything will turn out well and you get to go home at the end of the night.'

The other officers couldn't find any drugs in the location. The intel was flawed. The man we had chased down was just an illegal Mexican immigrant – like all the others, he'll simply be sent straight back to Mexico. We asked Jesse if he was disappointed.

He shrugged. 'Sure. But this is policing in this town. You gotta put your 100 per cent in because you really don't know who you're after at the time. Like I said, it could be someone who just murdered somebody or somebody that's been wanted or even someone in the top 10 most wanted. Or … it can be like this where it just turned out to be an illegal. It's still the job, right?'

He grinned, and wiped a big slick of sweat from his forehead. 'And hey, running after somebody … it's always an adrenaline rush. This is just regular work in Laredo. Regular work and then back out on patrol.'

☆   ☆   ☆

We'd been in Laredo for a week and we still hadn't met any real criminals – just a bunch of illegal immigrants and the over-cocky son of a Pistolero ganglord. Nor had we seen any narcotics to speak of. And this in a city supposedly on the front line of the war against drugs, America's last outpost against the lawlessness of the Mexican cartels? It didn't seem right, somehow.

Something had to be done. And there was always the one place in town, of course, where we knew we were guaranteed to find gangsters.

Laredo's top-security county jail is full to the brim with smugglers and killers. Just about everyone in here belongs to one gang or another – and those unlucky enough to find themselves behind these walls without a brotherhood to back them up either don't last long or quickly find themselves one.

Some of the top men are banged up here – and so deep and far-reaching are their criminal networks that some even manage to continue to run their business from their cells. In fact, as one of the cops warned us, there's probably more crime organised from the prisons than there is from the streets.

It wasn't the only warning we got. Before we were allowed to so much as see any inmates we got an hour's briefing from the man in charge here, Commander Juan Hernandez.

The first thing he did was explain the difference between the cartels and the gangs.

'The cartels belong to Mexico,' he said, 'and these gangs are home-grown, they belong here in this region. This is their area, gangs like the Pistoleros. Now, the Mexican mafia also has a strong presence here in the border – and so they control drugs along the border here, the sale of drugs and the collecting of taxes, to use a word, on other people's sale of drugs.'

The real problems have come, however, since the two parties started doing business together. 'The cartels are reaching out to these gangs because there's already a structure in place, see? They can utilise them and their structure to get whatever business they want to accomplish done. And that's either the movement of drugs or guns – or the elimination of targets.'

Some of the men in this prison were here for precisely that reason: eliminating targets. Murder. We wanted to know what the going rate for a hit was.

Hernandez shrugged. 'Depending on the target, anything from 10 thousand, to 50 thousand, to a Mercedes Benz, depending on who it may be. The cartels are not guys in suits and ties, they're criminals. And they rule by fear. Among the members and among the people they do business with. That's the bottom line.'

The commander didn't seem too enthusiastic about our presence in his jail: we got the impression that most of his briefing was designed to scare us off. And when it seemed clear we weren't going to back out, his final attitude seemed to be: if you want to do this, go ahead … but the consequences will be yours to deal with.

We asked him what those consequences might be.

'Well, the danger is that saying the wrong thing to the wrong person might get them killed,' he said. But that wasn't all. 'The danger to you is maybe that they're in jail for murder and things like that and, you know, making a name for themselves, putting a feather in their cap by striking a known person may be something that they won't think twice about.'

That was the real worry. Any sign of disrespect on our part, any feeling that we were being cheeky, or cocky, or that we had said anything that might drop someone in it … and someone could get hurt. Seriously. One of us even.

Did I want to meet these people so badly I was willing to risk their putting a hit on me? Christ, no. But I did it anyway.

We were led down a corridor that was straight out of *Silence of the Lambs*. Solid wall on one side, cells on the other, with floor-to-ceiling bars so that no part of them could be hidden from the wardens. Everything was painted white. Above us the dull buzz of the strip lighting was like the sound of bluebottles.

Some places just give off their own atmosphere – this place definitely did. Bad vibes were soaked through the walls here. We were on edge before we'd even walked 10 yards.

The first cell we stopped at held about eight people. Most looked pretty young – in their late teens, early twenties – and they stood with hands in pockets, staring straight at us, expressionless.

Slightly in front of them was an older guy with slicked black hair and a moustache. He nodded as we approached and a shiver went down my spine. I've met some scary men in my time, some big, bruising monsters on the pitch and off ... but this middle-aged man with the greasy hair trumped the lot of them. Even though he was behind bars and I was surrounded by cops, he gave me the creeps.

It turned out he was no stranger to prison – this time he was here on drug charges, looking at a 20-year stretch.

'When you get out,' I tried, 'the gangs on the outside ... do you have to go back into that gang, you can't get out of that?'

He shook his head, eyes locked straight into mine. 'I can't answer that question.'

OK.

'So ... what are the dangers out there for these young lads? Let's presume that one guy was into drugs, say?'

'Drugs?' he said, all fake shocked at the thought. 'That's the worst thing you can do, you know, get involved in drugs and smuggling and all that. You should know, that ain't no good, that's not going to take you nowhere. Over here you're dying, you know what I'm saying?'

Dying? 'So what would someone have to do on the street for them to, you know, whoever it is, to come and put them in a cemetery? What sort of things?'

He shrugged, his face still expressionless. 'I don't know, maybe you rip them off? You never know, it's hard to say, it's hard to answer. Say ... this guy maybe do something wrong and get pulled over and get busted – and you got pissed off with that and maybe put a hit on them. You know what I'm saying?'

Yes, we did. Loud and clear. No wonder they fought so hard to stay out of jail – it wasn't prison that scared them, it was the fact that simply getting arrested could mean someone taking out a contract on you. Either to stop you talking, or simply as revenge for losing them money. As far as the cartels are concerned, the lost merchandise is that much more valuable than someone's life.

We thanked him, wished him luck, and got the hell out of there.

※　※　※

Laredo hadn't turned out quite the way we thought it would. Sure, the evidence of multi-billion-dollar smuggling operations and ruthless Mexican drug cartels was all around – and in Jesse Jimenez we'd met an officer who was the physical embodiment of dedication, hard work and bravery ... but despite all that, the collars we'd made had not exactly turned out to be headline-grabbers.

But that's just it, of course. Headlines are headlines precisely because they don't happen that often. When you're a cop, it's the daily grind that matters, doing the job day after day with the same intensity and dedication, no matter what. This is their life. Cops like Jesse: they're human beings just trying to maintain law and order in whatever ways they have to, according to whatever circumstances they find themselves in. And it really is a game of cat and mouse: the good guys versus the bad guys. You've got one side chasing, the other side running.

What made it a little bit depressing was that it seemed to us that, despite their dedication, the cops in Laredo were fighting a losing battle – because even when they did catch these illegal immigrants, once they'd done the paperwork and driven them back over the border ... they knew that within 15 minutes they would be down by the riverside trying to get back across. It really is that simple.

It's not as if most of these immigrants even felt like real criminals. The smugglers are one thing – but their human cargo, for the most part, are just people trying to improve their lives. So many of them live in horrendous poverty back in Mexico – they're running away from that, running towards what they've always seen as the Promised Land. Is that so bad?

Cops like Jesse understand that. Half the time he's as much a social worker as he is a police officer: when he's not chasing suspects through pitch-black alleys with a semi-automatic rifle, he's listening to desperate people plead not to be sent back to their desperate lives.

So what can he do about it? Nothing. Keep working. Keep doing the job ... because every now and then the job will throw up something that really does make it all worthwhile.

* * *

We'd met our bad guys. All that was missing now was the drugs. And that's when Jesse came through for us.

When Jesse called on our last afternoon in the city we were glad to hear from him simply because we liked the guy ... but when we listened to what he had to say we liked him even more. He was speaking from the site of another busted stash house, on the east side of the city. The location wasn't the only difference – this time the building had given up the goods.

By the time we arrived the man guarding the place had already been taken away: predictably, it was Jesse who nailed him, chasing him across the backyard and tackling him, American football style. Once again, it was just his training kicking in, he said –

though on this occasion it turned out the suspect wasn't just another kid on the run ... and he wouldn't be going back to Mexico any time soon either.

Jesse met us at the door with a grin. 'Glad you guys could make it,' he said, and showed us through to the front room.

Inside, the place looked just like any other suburban home. None of your Mendoza flashiness here – and none of your temporary squat-type squalor either. It was a family residence: there were flowery curtains, neat crockery on the sideboard, clean carpets and well-kept furniture.

And on the dining table, a stack of parcels, each about A4 size and thick as airport novels, wrapped in brown paper and clingfilm.

'Cocaine,' said Jesse. 'Each one of these weighs approximately 2.2 pounds. Call each of them a kilo – a kilo of cocaine.'

What's the street value of a kilo of coke?

'Here in Laredo? About 15 thousand dollars,' he said, smiling as our eyes widened. That was cheap, right? He nodded. 'Fifteen thousand a kilo in Laredo, and yes, that's cheap. Up north, in the northern states, it can be anywhere from 30 to 45 a kilo.'

By the time it reached the UK, you'd be looking to pay 45 grand in sterling. Even at today's exchange rates, it's a significant mark-up – and that's before the stuff is cut. After it had been mixed and diluted down (with baking soda, paracetamol, corn starch, talcum powder, bleach even – your average coke dealer really isn't too fussy), we were looking at millions. Right there, on this kitchen table in this neat suburban family home, was more money than a lot of footballers or Hollywood actors make in a lifetime.

Jesse pointed to a tall cupboard in the corner of the kitchen. 'He had it up there, on top of the pantry. Being that the value is so high on these, usually they've been sent out from cartels in Mexico.'

He wasn't done yet, either. On the floor next to the sofa were a couple of breezeblock-sized bundles – again, wrapped up in clingfilm to hide the smell from the sniffer dogs at the border. 'That's marijuana,' he said. 'You're looking at roughly seven to 10 pounds; it's not weighed yet but it seems like it. That was found up in the attic.'

Upstairs there was another find. We followed Jesse into a bedroom: the undersized furniture, bright blue curtains and red walls covered in pictures of toy cars marked it out immediately as a little boy's room. We couldn't help noticing that amongst the usual dump trucks and diggers and fire engines there were plenty of cop cars too.

One of the sheriff's men showed us what they'd found in this room, hidden amongst the child's toys. A 22-calibre rifle, complete with sniper's scope. A nice final touch.

Make no mistake. This was a big score. These drugs wouldn't be making it to any street dealers … and somewhere, some serious bad guys were going to lose a lot of money. We couldn't help remembering what the man in the county jail had told us about the retribution dealt out to those whose stash gets busted: we shivered at the thought.

The haul was loaded into one of the cars and we prepared to move out. 'We're going to take it all back and test those packages to see if they come up positive for narcotics,' confirmed Jesse – though it was clear they would.

He looked pretty pleased with himself. We asked him how he felt. 'I feel good!' he said. 'It definitely feels good: taking drugs off the street feels good.'

As it turned out he had another reason for being happy. As we said our goodbyes he had one last thing to tell us. 'I got my promotion,' he grinned. 'I'm going to be an investigator with the criminal division.' It meant no more lonely shifts on Route 83, no more picking up sad border-dodgers.

'That's right,' he said. 'I work in narcotics now.'

MEAN STREETS: KEEPING THE PEACE WITH DONNY MOSES

Baltimore, Maryland, aka Bodymore, Murderland. Made infamous by gritty cop show *The Wire*, this former industrial port city on America's east coast now has the dubious honour of being known as murder capital, USA.

Downtown it's all shiny offices and tourist attractions, but head away from the waterfront and it's a different story. In the urban sprawl massive housing projects have been allowed to decay and deteriorate – and for many of those who live here society has fallen apart along with the buildings. Every week there are nearly 200 violent crimes and five murders in these urban wastelands, and 85 per cent of all homicides here are committed with guns.

It's a city with a crippling drugs problem where one person in every 10 is an addict. Drug-related offences are directly linked to over two-thirds of all crime in the city.

And guess what? I was getting in there amongst it all.

I don't mind confessing I didn't really know what to expect. Getting down there and dirty, on ground level, in the heat of the moment … anything could happen. Perhaps that's why I was so up for it.

Luckily I had the best partner a man could hope for. Detective Donny Moses grew up in the projects and has spent the last 15 years policing them, rolling – often alone – in his patrol car, chasing down guns and drugs, thieves and pushers, addicts and murderers, putting his life on the line every day. He knows these streets too well – and the streets know him right back.

I spent a four-till-midnight shift with Donny: and if it was a baptism of fire, it was also a crash course in street-level, front-line, urban policing.

❊ ❊ ❊

WE FIRST MET DONNY MOSES in the car park of a station in Baltimore's notorious West Side. There's only one district on the whole east coast of America that compares to it for crime levels – and that's Baltimore's East Side. Donny, as it turned out, patrolled them both.

He came out of the building with a kind of rolling swagger, pistol easy on the hip, baseball cap turned the wrong way round, bullet-proof vest over a sleeveless white T-shirt. He didn't look like a cop. He was cool. Too cool for school. If it wasn't for the gun and the Kevlar vest he could have passed for another guy in the hood … although, having said that, the boys in these hoods more than likely do come with pistols and bullet-proofs as standard.

He grinned his hellos and shook hands – and immediately it was like we'd known him for years. For the next eight hours we were going to be partners: he had to know we were solid – and from our point of view there were no concerns about him. Straight off we just knew that whatever Baltimore threw at us, Donny would have it covered. He radiated confidence. Not cockiness – but confidence, the kind you get from years of proving yourself, day after day after day. Up close he looked a little less like a 20-something street kid and a little more like a late-30-something police officer … but up close you could also appreciate the sheer presence of the guy.

He had a grip: when he shook hands you knew about it. And that easy confidence and laid-back attitude hid a serious physicality too. Donny was tough.

Kitting us out in bullet-proof vests – he handed them over with a shrug and a semi-apologetic smile, like he was giving us something he knew would make us uncomfortable but which at the end of the day we didn't really have any choice about – he introduced us to his partner and showed us into the car. We were shadowing Donny on patrol in both the East and West Sides of the city – and none of us knew what would be in store.

BALTIMORE

'This shift is basically the four-to-twelve shift,' he said as he pulled out of the lot and pointed his wheels straight into the afternoon sun, the heat of the day still radiating off the sidewalks and buildings, the air stifling, almost suffocating. 'We're about to ride around the streets, patrol Baltimore city for the next eight hours, see what happens. Just hope that people stay safe and keep people safe, keep the violence down.' He grinned again. 'You're here with us because this is one of the busy shifts in the department. In Baltimore everything pretty much shuts down at two a.m. So things die out in the early morning. But from four to twelve, people have got off from work, the kids are awake, the drug dealers, the junkies ... they're all awake. And right now they're all about to see what they can get into for the evening, see how much money they can make tonight. And we're out there to prevent them from doing what they do.'

As we cruised deeper into the projects the number of derelict properties increased, the boarded-up houses and shuttered shops began to creep up on the maintained buildings ... The streets looked quiet enough – there were lots of people around – but no one really seemed to be doing anything. No one was even moving too much.

Everyone was just kind of ... hanging out. On the corners by the grill-windowed liquor stores, leaning on railings or fire hydrants, or simply sitting on steps leading up to the houses. Some talked, some just sat and watched. The streets were riddled with people and they were all just sitting on their porches with nothing to do. They all looked bored stiff, to be honest.

And the heat was crushing. The heat, as it turns out, plays its own part in these places: it really gets to people. It creates its own tension. Heat and poverty and boredom ... it's a bad recipe. It can cause serious friction.

Donny had the air-con on full but the windows wound down: you see better that way, he explained; you see clearer. The windows stay open in the heavy heat of summer and they stay open in the freezing depths of winter. As we moved, his head swivelled; his eyes went everywhere, on the streets themselves and the alleys that disappeared off them, locking on to each face we passed, scoping the body language.

We asked him what he was looking for exactly.

'Well, anything, to be honest,' he admitted. 'Me, I am a drug cop by trade; I seem to catch all the hand-to-hand transactions. I'm just looking for any type of criminal activity … and of course if you look long enough you find, you see.'

He waved an arm out of the window. 'As you guys can see, a lot of people are just hanging out here – and not all of them are bad. As a police officer you have to tell who are the bad guys and who are the good people that are just hanging out. It can be tough; we make mistakes.

'I always take notice of the people that don't want to look at me back. Normally those are the ones to watch, those who go the extra mile not to get noticed. Everybody who has a reason for not being noticed – I want to know what that reason is.

'The funny thing is when you are in these neighbourhoods you can't turn it off. You never turn it off.'

We looked again at the people on their porches as we passed, watching us watching them. Most of the houses here were derelict now; the street looked like a smashed-in mouth, the empty windows like so many missing teeth. And nobody seemed especially pleased to see us.

Donny didn't mind about that. These were his streets. If, to our eyes, everyone looked like trouble, he saw a little deeper than that. As he talked we realised something: he may be a cool guy, but he's also deep. He's a bit of a philosopher is our Don, he's thought long and hard about a lot of things and arrived at a few truths along the way. As we rolled through the neighbourhoods he laid it all out for us.

'The bad people,' he said, 'not all of them are bad all the way down. These are hard times, and not everybody has the financial means to live at least something like a quality life … so they resort to negative things to try and equal out the odds. You got people out here who sell drugs – and that has always been a bad trade. And of course wherever you have drugs you have violence, you have the guns. And those who don't sell, just take what don't belong to them, break into property.

'Guns are too easy to come by here in Baltimore city. Everyone has a gun, unfortunately. We have guns; they have guns. We all have guns. People who aren't looking to do wrong – even they have guns just to protect themselves. And the way I see it is, if you don't have a gun then you are more prone to walk away from a violent situation. But then if you do have a gun, you have that false sense of confidence. And of course, a lot of people say, well I have it so I may as well use it … and that's when things get really bad.'

He turned and flashed a grin again. 'We'll see what happens in Baltimore tonight. I got a feeling it's gonna be a warm night.'

✺   ✺   ✺

Donny Moses had not been our first port of call in this city. We'd arrived with our heads full of *The Wire* and with pages of research material full of frightening statistics. As well as the murder rates and sky-high violent crime levels, as well as the cold facts that 10 per cent of Baltimore's inhabitants are addicts and that their drug habits account for 66 per cent of all crime here, we'd seen enough episodes of *The Wire* to understand that the city's troubles were far deeper than that.

In the TV drama, the problems went way beyond a few rough areas on the edges of society – it showed that guns and drugs have become a part of the fabric of Baltimore. And it also showed that the police were all but helpless before the sheer scale of the crisis: for every good cop making a good bust there were 50 bad guys trying to take him down … and 50 more waiting behind them. *The Wire* is a great show, but it's not, let's be fair, anything like a good advert for the city – or even, despite the heroics of the cops featured, for the Baltimore Police Department.

But at the end of the day it is just another TV show, right? It's drama. It's not real. We wanted to be sure – because there was, after all, no arguing with the statistics. We wanted to know why this town is being so overrun by drugs and guns and just what the police have to do to keep law and order here. And we reckoned the best place to start was at the very top.

A meeting was set up with Commissioner of Police Frederick Bealefield. He's the boss round here – and he has the experience and the smarts to match his title. Bealefield's grandfather, great-grandfather and great-uncles were all on the force: he became a cadet immediately after leaving high school in 1981 and over the last 28 years has worked his way up through the ranks the hard way.

His first four years on the job were spent walking foot patrol in the Western district, the next 13 years working homicide. Since then it's been one promotion after another – and now he's the one deciding exactly how the cops try to tackle the crime epidemic here.

His solution is radical.

He has abandoned the zero tolerance policy now adopted by most forces in favour of a specific targeting of what he considers to be the root of all the problems. Funnily enough, it was the same conclusion Donny had come to: guns.

'Fifty per cent of all the people charged with murder in this city every year had prior gun offences,' he told us – and he wants to do something about it. The way Bealefield sees it, Baltimore's chronic drug addiction has its roots in guns, and continues to thrive only because of guns.

Which is not to say that he's being soft on the pushers. Even for a first-time offender the punishment is harsh: the jail term can be anything from 10 to 40 years depending on the amount of drugs involved. But the bottom line is it simply doesn't deter the dealers, as many of them choose to offend again. On just one street in Baltimore an estimated 10 million dollars can be made dealing drugs every year.

And a gun is the only sure-fire way of protecting that money.

Naturally this filters down to cops like Donny. With almost 4,000 assaults on officers every year in the state, body armour is absolutely essential for all cops in the field – and the threat of getting shot is a daily reality.

Bealefield wants to battle back. He's mobilising to wage war on the gun-wielding bad guys – but even he knows the odds are stacked against him.

'Bad guys with guns, they get out of jail, you know what they do?' he asked us. 'They get guns again. We take them off them but it's like trying to count grains of sand on a beach. There's 30,000 on the streets – and in a good year we will seize 4,000 guns. Four thousand. They sold 30,000. You will never keep up; you can't even keep up with what they sold.

'There are prisons full of guys for drugs. We lock up drug deal-ers by the basket-full. But you know what?' He leant forward over his desk and looked us straight in the eye. 'I would trade any one them for a guy with a gun.'

✤ ✤ ✤

Back on the front line with Donny and he was taking us on a history trip.

We were deep in the West Side now, and as the sun set over the terraced houses and tired looking low-rises, everything was bathed in a gold and red light, the last of the rays giving these sad streets a kind of beauty. It was still hot as hell, though – and we couldn't help noticing that the dying day seemed to bring more people out on to the sidewalks and porches.

Donny idled the car on a corner and gestured towards one group; some standing, some sitting on the steps up to another empty building. All were in their twenties, in long shorts and basketball tops, loose and easy with the confidence only street kids have.

One had a telltale brown bag, from which they took it in turns to take sips. By US law you're not allowed to drink alcohol in the streets … hence the practice of keeping your booze wrapped in the bag in which you bought it. Of course, the cops know that anyone swigging from a paper bag is probably not going to be hiding Coca-Cola – but it's a kind of unwritten rule on the streets that so long as the drinkers are at least making the effort to conceal their drinks, the cops tend not to do too much about it.

There's even a segment of an episode in *The Wire* on the 'brown bag issue' – one of the characters calls the whole unspoken agreement 'a great moment of civic compromise'.

We couldn't help noticing they were passing around a home-rolled cigarette too – which, let's be honest, is not usually a sign that they're short on tobacco. As we waited across the street, they waved. One of them shouted something we didn't pick up: the others collapsed in laughter.

Donny ignored them. They were small fry, nobodies, not worth the sweat. A bottle of booze; a suspect smoke? Whatever. And besides, they weren't the reason we'd pulled over. He wanted to point out something more important. This was where Donny grew up.

'See where these boys are sitting?' he said, indicating the group. 'That's where my grandmother lived. All these houses, none of them were vacant then. My babysitter used to live some-where across here when I was a little boy ...' He studied each of the houses, frowning. 'I don't remember which one. This place used to be a beauty salon ... and this place' – he pointed at a glorified pile of rubble – 'this was my first church.'

But Donny didn't just grow up here – he worked these streets. Fifteen years ago, as a raw recruit straight out of the academy, Donny Moses was assigned this neighbourhood of West Baltimore ... and spent the following nine summers busting deals, taking down gangsters and running the gauntlet every single day.

Round here there's no jobs, no opportunities, no legitimate money to be made. Kids from the projects rarely graduate from high school – and even if they do, what are they going to do then? Flog-ging yourself to make enough to scrape the rent is a sucker's game in the projects, even if you could find someone willing to give you work. Far easier to get into drugs. With one in 10 citizens of this city an addict, there's a massive, eager and willing market for narcotics. And for too many young people from the West Side, supplying that demand looks like the only real option open to them.

Donny's the exception. But he's also the exception who proves the rule.

'This corner's a famous corner,' he grinned. 'West Bal-ti-more' – he said it in a singsong lilt; and he shook his head with a look that was a strange mix of regret, nostalgia and even something like pride. 'Historically this is a high drug area. Whatever you want: heroin, crack cocaine … you could buy it here, back in the late 80s right up through the 90s. It's pretty quiet now, though.

'But this place is famous for me anyway. This was my first post when I became a police officer. And I was wet behind the ears then, I didn't know a lot about narcotics. But as it turned out narcotics has been pretty much my career. It's what I was good at. And I am proud of it, I am proud because it is quieter here now and I had something to do with that.

'There was a lot of drug dealing in this particular area. At one time they were making so much money around here, it would be literally like going to an open market. Some afternoons it was like buying fruit and veg, y'know? You would see lookouts, addicts on every corner. You would see young kids and old people. You would see people coming from different neighbourhoods. People from different cities even. White or black, it didn't matter: this was the place to get your drugs.'

But it was in this area that Donny learnt his trade – and established a reputation for himself. The way he told it was like he was reminiscing about schooldays, good times; speaking in his easy tone, half smiling all the time … it was easy to forget he was talking about serious crime – and serious danger.

We asked him exactly what his job as a rookie narco involved. He fired up the car and set off again, pointing out streets and alleyways as we passed them.

'I was famous for creeping through the alleys,' he laughed. 'A lot of times I would just walk out the alleys. And I could just sit on those steps. People would not even notice me; I would sit and just watch them. Just hand-to-hand selling drugs.

'Of course, I was considerably younger then and properly looked younger, y'know? So it was easy for me to just sneak through the holes. Avoid the lookouts, the people looking out for police. All these buildings are pretty abandoned now, but we would climb up the fire escapes, lay on the rooftops. A lot of the times they would put their drugs in these drainpipes. If I was laying under one of those porches they would never notice, so all I had to do is remember basically who put it there. Then I would call in my partners, give out the description of the dealers. They would stop them on the streets and I would give them the drugs right here. I would just pick drug dealers off and they would always wonder how they got caught.' He laughed again. 'So we had a lot of tactics, we worked a lot of ways.'

It was about as basic as undercover policing can get. Donny was front-line, ground-level, mixing with the bad guys daily, breathing their same air. And for nine years? We couldn't believe he'd gotten away with it so long. Appropriately enough, he had exactly the right story for us. Pulling the car over again, he indicated a block of houses opposite a vacant lot.

'Well,' he said, 'this here block was also the scene of my first fight. I had seen somebody dealing drugs. And this one guy, he was about six foot three, 240 to 250 pounds … and he had about 50 people around him. He had a bag in his hand and he was dealing the drugs, and like a dummy I ran to the middle of the crowd. The guy hit me in the mouth and ran off. I chased him down into this block and then at this point the fight was on. But then everybody that was out here starting throwing bottles at me – because I was throwing bottles at him. When he realised he could not outrun me he turned right in the middle of the street to fight me.

He was bigger then me and my mouth was all bloody. But I didn't even think about the size, I just went straight for him.

'Anyways, so obviously you know I won, right? I placed him under arrest and then I dealt with the bottle and rock throwers as well. That incident pretty much gave me my reputation. They said about me: you know he's little and soft-spoken but he is not to be tested.' He laughed again and moved the car on once more. 'And the rest is history, right? Here we are. Back in West Bal-ti-more.'

Here we were. Donny's credentials were established beyond all doubt. The man was just about as straight-up street-smart as anyone I'd met, and now we knew he had the history to back up the cool ... but what next? We still hadn't seen Donny in action.

That was about to change.

✻ ✻ ✻

It didn't take long before the history lesson was over and reality replaced theory. The sun still hadn't set when the first serious call of the shift came through.

The radio crackled and within seconds Donny had hit the siren and we were screaming through the streets en route to a domestic. The details were sketchy: all we knew was that a young man was apparently threatening his parents – why exactly was unclear. It could be drugs, it could be money, it could be something as stupid as an argument over whose turn it was to do the washing up. But with around one fatal shooting a week within family homes in this state, the whys and wherefores were not exactly Donny's priority right then. What was important was getting there before anyone got killed.

We pulled up at the same time as another patrol car and Donny was moving before we could even ask permission to follow. Warn-

TOP Sherriff's man Jesse Jimenez: 'Only my mom calls me Jesus...'

ABOVE LEFT Patrolling the Rio Grande between Texas and Mexico – can you guess which of these three men isn't the trained police officer?

ABOVE RIGHT Last minute instructions before the SWAT raid in Laredo as the team prepared for a 'hard entry' – striking fast and without warning.

ABOVE Suspect Mendoza Junior considers his options as the SWAT team ransack his house for drugs and guns.

LEFT A moment's reflection with the Laredo SWAT: 'We will do whatever it takes to maintain stability and safety in our community. And the cost at times is the ultimate sacrifice.'

TOP LEFT Donny Moses: too cool for school.

TOP RIGHT Donny ribs me about my shooting skills. 'Any mean-looking dogs need taking out, I know who to radio in – dead or alive, right Vinnie?'

ABOVE Donny made his reputation in Baltimore's worst areas: 'I was famous for creeping through alleys – they said about me: you know he's little and soft spoken but he is not to be tested.'

TOP Crack shots – posing with the boys at the Baltimore firing range.

ABOVE LEFT I couldn't really miss from this distance, could I?

ABOVE RIGHT Getting a lesson in street-level survival from a veteran: every week there are nearly 200 violent crimes and five murders on the streets of Baltimore.

TOP LEFT Sergeant Apollos Terry – the blood on his shirt is not his own.

TOP RIGHT Welcome to the Jungle: in Papua New Guinea, criminals often hide in the impenetrable highlands. Going after them means learning to survive in the wild.

ABOVE LEFT The Royal PNG Constabulary sends a million quid's worth of marijuana up in smoke.

ABOVE RIGHT There's barely a senior officer here without some kind of scar to show for it.

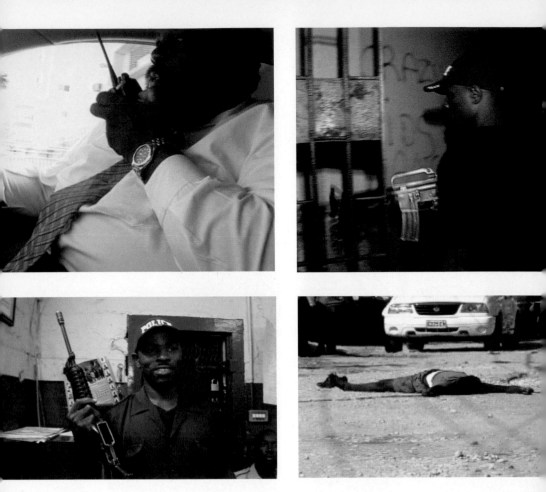

TOP LEFT Bigga Ford racing to another murder scene: 'When the place is mashed up only he can bring it back.'

TOP RIGHT The ghettos of Kingston are a virtual no-go zone for cops – M16 rifles come as standard issue.

ABOVE LEFT Corporal Byron Lewis: 'There's a thin line between a fool and bravery. If shots are raining down and you want to walk out in it, I wouldn't say it's bravery – that's stupidity.'

ABOVE RIGHT Face down in the dust – another of the 1,500 murder victims a year in Jamaica.

TOP Sergeant Ron Lopez: in LA, even the cops look like movie stars.

ABOVE LEFT Another teenage crack peddler arrested. Drug seizures in LA are up by as much as 1,000 per cent – because the cops are confiscating more ... and because there's so much more out there to confiscate.

ABOVE LEFT This kid's off the streets for a while – but his long-term prospects aren't good. In South Central LA boys as young as 13 are out pushing drugs for the gangs.

ABOVE Ron, Steve McLean and I discuss football and dog racing after another drug bust.

ings were shouted, and cops from both cars busted open the front door almost simultaneously; within seconds they had all dived in. We followed. It wasn't difficult to find the source of the problem – from the kitchen at the back of the house all hell was breaking loose: a man's voice shouting, raw, desperate; a woman scream-ing. Donny's team were all over them almost before the people realised they were there at all.

The scene didn't look good: one man in his twenties, wild-eyed, jumpy, yelling at the top of his voice; another man – his father, presumably – cowering in the corner; and an elderly woman, screaming, too close to the offender.

More warnings. Hands on holsters. More screaming. The man's arms too active, his actions too hostile. A final warning. And then ...

Suddenly he made a move, grabbing his mother (or grand-mother, aunty, who knew?), pulling her to him, snatching at her arm, trying to lock his hand around her neck ... Donny's men had had enough. A final warning and then something was pulled from a holster, aimed, fired.

Almost in silence, the man spasmed and keeled over, like he'd been swatted by an enormous, invisible hand. Flat on the floor he twitched and shook, his legs and arms jerking like he'd been elec-trified.

Which, as it turned out, he had. At that time around 50,000 volts of electricity were coursing through his body, taking out his nerv-ous system, disabling him as effectively as if he'd been shot straight through the heart. The difference, of course, was that after a few minutes he was going to be perfectly fine again.

But by then the handcuffs were on and the whole incident was effectively over.

One of Donny's colleagues had employed a taser device – shooting the suspect with two hooked wires, designed to penetrate clothing and with barbs to stick in his flesh. Through those wires the massive electrical charge was delivered: immediately incapacitating him.

We'd heard about these before, of course – that boy with the chicken in New Orleans had been tasered – but this was the first time we'd seen one used up close.

It wasn't pretty, seeing a man flapping around on the floor like a drowning fish – but as Donny pointed out, it was an awful lot better than seeing him lying stone still in a pool of his own blood. And it was infinitely better than seeing any police officer bleed.

'This young man apparently was giving his family members a problem,' he shrugged, as the suspect was stretchered into an ambulance and other officers interviewed the victims to try to establish exactly what the dispute was all about. 'We tried to gain control of him, tried to talk him out of his rage … but it didn't appear to work. Ultimately we had to tase him, use less-than-lethal force. And once we tased him, we handcuffed him and it was over.'

After the suspect had been checked out by the paramedics and given the all-clear, he was taken to hospital to have the taser prongs removed … and straight from there to the station, to be charged with assaulting a police officer.

Rough justice? It could have been an awful lot rougher. According to the makers, 170,000 suspects are tasered across the US every year. As a non-lethal response and an alternative to the gun, it's a no-brainer for the cops.

But for cops like Donny, using a taser is a luxury they don't often have. In this city of guns, fire is best fought with fire.

✵   ✵   ✵

BALTIMORE

Following our meeting with Commissioner Bealefield, there was only one place we were going to go. So guns were Baltimore's number one problem, and number one target, and number one way of dealing with that problem? So we'd better learn how to fire one.

We had a date on the firing range.

Tasers are useful enough in situations like domestic arguments – anything, in fact, where you've got a clear line of sight and nobody's waving anything too deadly around – but the grim reality is that on any given shift an officer in Baltimore is going to be reaching for his pistol more often than for any less-than-lethal alternative.

I've handled a few firearms before, but ducks and clay pigeons aren't much of a preparation for what these boys are facing every day. To try to understand just a little of what cops like Donny have to put themselves through just to stay alive, some serious coaching in quick thinking and instant response was called for ... as well as finding out what it feels like to handle a real weapon. At the Baltimore police firearms training facility, an officer took time out to put me through my paces. The exercise was exactly the same as for all the cops – and it was designed to show officers how to deal with hostile problems on the street.

But the days of flip-up cardboard bad guys are well over. This is the PlayStation and Xbox age – and firearms training in Baltimore has embraced the new technology. We were to be using a simulator which plays out shootout scenarios: a bit like a video game, one of those first-person shooters, it involves standing in front of a giant screen holding a gun exactly the same weight and calibre as standard police issue. The only difference is that there are no real bullets: you shoot at the screen and you only find out afterwards how well you did.

This is where the training comes in; this is where the hours are racked up. Crack-shot officers on the street only become so thanks to the time spent in front of screens like this. To use a football analogy, if the cop on the street taking out the bad guy with a single shot is like David Beckham landing a perfect free kick … then this is where all the hard work is done to make sure that when it matters, he hits the target. Becks on the training ground, the Baltimore PD right here. Practice, practice, practice.

Sadly, it's been a long time since I've done much practice at either football or shooting – and I don't mind admitting that I've never been as accurate as David Beckham. On top of that, I think the officer overseeing training that day wasn't exactly loving having to look after a bunch of British guys.

'Right, this is a firearms training system,' he said. He was getting on a bit, with grey hair and more than a few extra pounds round his waist. 'We bring recruits in here, and we bring our officers in here.' He handed us the gun: it was surprisingly heavy. 'This is basically the same kind of weapon that we carry on the streets,' he continued. 'This is a Glock model 22, 40 calibre. So, you just aim and …' He pointed at the screen and unleashed a volley at the video. The man who had a second before been trying to make off with a telly now lay crumpled on the floor. He didn't look like he was ever going to get back up.

'You ever shoot?' he asked, looking more than a little pleased with his handiwork. 'Good. Let me see you do it.'

He reset the video and a new scenario popped up. A woman and a man were in a room – she seemed to be holding him hostage, or maybe he was holding her, there was a blind lady there too, she had a guide dog, or … suddenly something happened. There was a push, the woman had a gun, she was pointing it straight at us – instinct took over and I gave her everything I had, spraying a few shots at the mutt for good measure.

The officer in charge was not happy.

'Whaddya shoot the dog for?' he shouted. 'The machine says you're not supposed to shoot the dog! And secondly, that dog's on a leash – it can't even hurt you.' He hit the replay button and the pattern of bullets showed up. The dog was dead all right; the bitch was still alive. 'She got you,' he said, shaking his head. 'Let's see if you did hit her …'

A series of red Xs came on the screen. As suspected, most had missed the suspect, though one had dealt her a glancing blow. The Labrador was toast.

'Missed her, missed her, got her,' he said, pointing to each marker. 'That's a non-incapacitating hit, though – that means she's not gonna go down … and then she got you and it's all over. Most police shootings are over in three to five seconds: it's boom boom and it's over. You didn't even see her draw that gun, did you? Yeah, you need some training all right.'

Considering it was my first time his assessment seemed a bit harsh. 'You know, in the movies,' I said, 'even if you miss them they still go down.'

He shook his head and turned away. 'I hate movies,' he muttered.

❈   ❈   ❈

We told Donny about it. He laughed. 'Any mean-looking dogs need taking out, I know who to radio in,' he said. 'Dead or alive, right Vinnie?'

It was just about the last laugh of the night.

As darkness had fallen we'd switched districts. Leaving the West Side to look after itself, we'd turned our back on the setting sun and headed East. Donny called it one of the worst places on the east coast, in terms of crime and violence. 'But,' he pointed out, raising a finger, 'the guys are doing a good job over here. Don't forget that.'

We wouldn't. We'd see for ourselves.

On the way across the city we'd stopped for a bite to eat. The cops here have got two or three places they exclusively use … for reasons that would become clear. As it turned out we were miles from any of them, and so Donny pulled into a 7–11. Dinner was going to be cold sandwiches.

We asked him why not any one of the fast-food places – at least get something hot inside us? The reason was devastatingly simple. Cops in Baltimore only eat where the food is sealed – or where they can see it being prepared. You never know what they're going to do to your burger and fries if you're not looking.

After the heat of the day, the cool of the evening brought a darker side of the city on to the streets. When the sun goes down in Baltimore the monsters come out. It's what makes this four-till-twelve shift the busy shift. It's what makes it the most dangerous.

It didn't take long before we got our next call. A ranking officer had radioed for back-up – the details were sketchy but it seemed kids with guns were involved. Most cops in this city ride solo, relying on back-up to help out when they need it. It's a system that works … but it also means that when a call for assistance comes in, the first instinct is to assume the worst.

Donny hit the sirens, put the pedal to the metal and screwed his baseball cap on tighter. The call sounded urgent to him: he wasn't taking any chances.

As it turned out we were not the first to arrive. By the time we screamed up, the streets were lit up in blue and red flashing lights, cops everywhere, patrol cars scattered across the road. Donny jumped out and shouldered his way through to the most senior-looking officer he could find. They chatted for a while, Donny doing most of the listening, nodding, before smiling and shaking the cop's hand.

It seems that a patrol car had spotted someone they didn't like the look of, had pulled over, challenged him … and the boy had pulled a gun. The officer hadn't flinched – he pulled one back. The kid did probably the only sensible thing he'd done for years: he tossed the weapon. But then he went and ruined it all by trying to outrun the police.

He was face down over the car's bonnet now, legs spread, arms handcuffed behind his back, two uniformed cops asking him questions. Dressed in standard homeboy uniform – the long shorts, the baggy T-shirt, the spotless white trainers – he also looked young. Too young to be here; way too young to be in possession of a lethal firearm. Put it this way: I wouldn't have served the kid a beer back in England, never mind letting him loose on the streets with a Smith and Wesson.

On the roof of the car lay the gun in question.

Donny filled us in. 'This is the gun that they got off the suspect,' he said. 'Like I said, they got out on a guy they expected to be armed, when they jumped out he took off running, he was quickly apprehended and the gun was recovered. We're not gonna touch it but you can see it's loaded with at least six rounds.' He peered a little closer, shining his torch over the barrel. It was a big beast of a thing, bigger than the standard-issue shooters we'd been practising with earlier. It also looked in immaculate condition – which meant one of two things. Either it had never been used at all … or the kid was such a professional he took pride in keeping his piece squeaky clean.

Looking at his face – more fear than defiance there, and with none of that cynicism and cockiness we'd see so many times from those used to being caught in possession – we were putting our money on the first theory. We could only hope we were right.

'He didn't discharge the weapon,' Donny went on, 'but just the fact that he had it on him, that he tried to get rid of it when he noticed the police on him … that ain't good for him. And that's a 9mm semi-automatic pistol … Some guys get revolvers, other guys get semi-automatic weapons, it's regular in this part of town.' He shook his head. 'It's regular all over this city.'

The bottom line is the same, though: any gun off the street is a good result for the cops.

We left them to it and got back in the car – and the handbrake was barely off before Donny was back on the radio, speaking low and urgently, listening to the operator's rapid-fire responses.

Siren on. Foot down. 'It's a warm night in Bal-ti-more,' he chanted as we gained speed again. And things were getting hotter.

Gunfire had been heard in an alley deep in the East Side – Donny took the call and we were marked down as on it. We'd be investigating alone for the moment, but any trouble and back-up wouldn't be far off.

It was pitch black now – even the buildings were shuttered up. We couldn't tell if they'd been abandoned, if they were simply closed for the night, or if, like in the old Western movies, the owners had barricaded themselves in once they'd heard the guns go off. In this area all three were possibilities.

We got out of the car in silence. Donny held his gun in one hand, his torch in the other, keeping both together, always pointed in the same direction, at the same target. If he could see something, he could shoot it.

We followed him at a good distance as he crept through the alley, crouched low, side-on, gun and torch sweeping the bushes, trees, walls and buildings. There wasn't a sound; everything was still. It was eerie – we were in the heart of the city and the place was deathly quiet.

He moved all the way down; all the way back. And then he did it again. And again. Finally, he stood up. The place was empty. It was quiet because no one was here. Either the shooter had got away – or there wasn't a shooter in the first place. The Fourth of July wasn't far off, and Donny had a theory about that.

'Bullets, fireworks, they both go bang, it's hard to tell the difference. But nonetheless you gotta take every necessary precaution. We take a call like this seriously because a lot of times when you hear of a discharge of firearms you actually find you have a victim. There was what sounded like two shots coming from this way. We did a quick canvas to make sure nobody actually has a gun back here.

'We're running into a dark alley here, low visibility and you gotta be prepared for somebody either in the high grass here or coming from around the corner or out of a backyard. They have no fear for themselves, let alone the police. If there had been a shooter here it would have been very dangerous. Nobody's afraid to shoot at or hurt police any more.'

Was he relieved, or was he disappointed? It was difficult to tell. After 15 years, it's all just become part of the job. The important thing is to stay safe, stay alive.

Donny reminded us that he was just a little player in a massive game. All over Baltimore other patrols were responding to similar calls. Some, like this, might be false alarms. Some, like the last, the kid with the big shiny gun, might be good busts. Others, as we were going to see, might just be too late. Any average four-till-twelve shift is going to get a good proportion of all three – and you can multiply that by every cop on duty, every night of the year.

It made me think of a city under attack, constantly, from the

inside. Like a cancer. All the cops can do is shoot from one incident to the next, hoping to get there in time, most times.

The next call didn't fall into that category. We were not there in
time.

❈   ❈   ❈

It was late now, past the hour when good boys and girls should
be tucked up in bed. We'd been on the streets for nearly a full
shift, but Donny was about to get one more job before he clocked
off for the night. And this one was very real.

As we raced back through the streets, Donny explained the situation.

'Apparently a call just came out for a shooting and armed
carjacking,' he said. 'One of the victims supposedly got shot in the
face. At this point we don't know much, the call has only been out
for five minutes, detectives haven't had the chance to get on the
scene yet to evaluate what's happened or the seriousness of it.
But we know at least one person's been shot.'

We got there just after the ambulances. Unlike the last area, this
was a busy road – noisy, well-lit, with cars constantly zooming by.
It didn't look the kind of place someone could get shot. Appearances, obviously, can be deceptive.

There were two men lying on the sidewalk, both surrounded
by paramedics. As we watched, one was lifted carefully on to a
stretcher and slid into the back of the ambulance. We couldn't see
his face – it was covered in bandages. They couldn't have been on
more than a few minutes, but already even we could see they
needed changing: the whole front of his head was a sodden, pulpy
red mess. We'd barely arrived when the door was slammed, the
siren screamed and he was on his way to the emergency room.

He wasn't the only victim. The other man was face down, half in the gutter, his feet bare – his Adidas trainers lay six or seven feet away. Whatever had hit him had literally blown his socks off.

It wasn't difficult to work out where he'd been shot. The back of his shorts were stained a deep, dark red. It may not have been as immediately life-threatening as catching a barrel full in the face – but if I had to choose to take a bullet anywhere, up my arse would not be in the top five options, that's for sure.

Donny was already heading for the remaining ambulancemen, raising a hand in salute to another patrol car that swung in to join us. 'All right,' he called back at us. 'You stay here. Now I gotta do my thing.'

We watched as he leant over the wounded man, patting him gently on the shoulder, talking all the while with the medics and the newly arrived back-up, occasionally leaning in to ask the victim a question.

We could hear his answers from where we were. The pain, the shock, plus whatever painkillers he'd been given, had made him weirdly lucid – though half-delirious, he was shouting his answers in a manic, edgy voice. By the time Donny rejoined us we knew almost as much as he did.

The two guys had been driving through this area, barely a block away from where we now stood, when their BMW had been stopped at gunpoint and they were ordered out. So what did they do? They did what any sensible person would do, what the police probably recommend you do – they complied. They got out.

They got shot anyway.

His mate took it first, smack in the face – and as this guy turned and tried to run he caught his bullet where the sun don't shine. The car was gone.

'These are the only two victims,' confirmed Donny. 'One victim was shot in the face. This victim was shot in the buttocks area … at this time neither victim is believed to be suffering from a life-threatening injury.' He waved an arm at two new cars that had pulled up. 'However, our district detective units are on the scene investigating this matter as we speak.'

Cut and dried then, right? Find the car and find the shooters? He pulled a face – 15 years on these streets had taught Donny Moses never to accept anyone's story at face value. Call it cynicism – or call it good policing.

'We're still not sure what to think,' he admitted. 'We got two different stories from both victims. They said they were carjacked in this area but we don't know yet. These detectives are going to start investigating, trying to get to the bottom of it. So, same as always, only time will tell.

'When a shooting has already occurred, the danger's done. The suspects have fled the scene and now all we have to do is come in and put the pieces of the puzzle together. It's a different kind of policing, right? So this type of scene is not so dangerous for us. It's the ones where the shootings haven't occurred yet, the threat level is high, where we are looking for the bad guys with the guns … they're the dangerous ones.'

He grinned at us. 'So how you guys like your first shift? We got you a gun tonight, we got you a shooting …'

It was gone midnight, time for shift change. Another day and night in Baltimore clocked up, another eight hours on the front line survived. There was only one place Donny was going now – and we definitely weren't invited.

We met a lot of stand-up guys in forces all over the world, but of all of them Donny was just about the easiest to get along with. When you talk about real tough guys you think of someone who's six foot six, built like a brick shithouse … which Donny isn't. But he's tougher than most of them. Donny's been there and done it all. He's probably seen more and done more than any gangster out there. For a decade and a half he's been in the firing line every single day – hustling pushers on street level in the West Side or responding to shootings on the East.

Are the bad guys putting themselves in the firing line every day? Of course not. But Donny is. And he's doing it because he wants this city to be better than it is.

Before he dropped us off, there was one final thing we wanted to get to the bottom of. How did he do it? What kept him sharp, on edge?

He shrugged, took off his baseball cap and then replaced it back to front, homeboy style again. 'To be honest with you, when I'm reacting to a situation nothing's going through my head except for what's right there in front of me. This is one of those jobs where if you think slow, think wrong, then you could be in trouble.

'But it's that nervousness that keeps you alive, keeps you sharp. The smart cops respect the streets; the smart cops respect their own instincts, their own fears and their own nervousness. I'm not saying you should let your fears govern you. You can't let your fears control you … but you should listen to your fears.

'Adrenaline is a drug, right? And once it starts running it runs and a lot of times it carries you through those nervous situations. The funny thing is, we Baltimore cops are kinda crazy because when people start shooting, instead of running away from the gunshots, we run towards them.

'Things happen quick in this line of work, things happen quick … you blink and next thing you know it's like, oh hell, all hell has broken loose.'

WELCOME TO THE JUNGLE: RAIDS AND BUSTS WITH APOLLOS TERRY

When Papua New Guinea was put forward as a destination for the first series of *World's Toughest Cops*, the initial reaction amongst some of the crew was disbelief. Papua New Guinea? The place is a paradise! A country of barely six million people, many still living a traditional tribal life in the wild tropical jungles; an ancient culture untouched by the worst excesses of the West …

Forget about it. In the last decade there has been an explosion of crime here. Gangs from the highlands and jungles have invaded the capital Port Moresby, bringing with them crime and violence on a previously unimaginable scale. The law of the jungle has come to the city: so much so that Port Moresby was recently voted the worst place to live in the world.

Battling to contain the chaos is the local police force – and foremost among them Sergeant Apollos Terry, a man built like an ex-heavyweight boxer and with a reputation as fearsome as any of the men he's up against.

We were here to shadow Apollos and his CID unit: and what we saw was eye-opening, to say the least. The respect and fatherly devotion that Apollos inspired in his men was matched by a vicious hatred from the criminals themselves. We would see both sides of the man … and, strangest of all, we would see just how that contradiction impacted on his own family life.

❖   ❖   ❖

PORT MORESBY CID HEADQUARTERS is not the most impressive building in the world. Just about the only solid-looking thing about it is the massive iron gates blocking the entrance. Behind them is a car park, mostly empty; and beyond that, Boroko police station. Right in the heart of the city, this should be the shiny, bustling nerve centre of the country's crime-busting operation – the Papua New Guinea equivalent of London's New Scotland Yard, or Washington's J. Edgar Hoover Building. Instead it looks more like an abandoned school. Crumbling walls, peeling paint, flaking woodwork and a very dodgy-looking roof.

The locks seem strong enough, however. They have to be: Papua New Guinea has a bit of a problem with criminals breaking out of prison. It seems to happen a lot in this country – according to some, maybe a bit too often for the blame to fall solely on the buildings themselves.

We were stopped at the gate by police officers holding big machine-guns and bigger frowns. That all changed once we told them who we were here to meet. Suddenly it was all smiles and they waved us through with thumbs up. It seems Sergeant Apollos Terry is a bit of a hero around here.

Part father figure, part mentor, part one-man force in his own right, Apollos heads up the Port Moresby CID unit. He's a big man, in every sense of the word. Big like a prize-fighter gone slightly to seed – and big in reputation too. He's the officer every young cop looks up to: and he's the man the criminals fear the most.

He met us with a huge smile, dressed simply in trousers and shirt. They don't really do ties and jackets in this country – and, despite the combats and armoured vests of the other cops around, Apollos doesn't tend to go for the intimidating look either. He doesn't need to.

After 23 years in the force, nothing fazes him. He's seen it all, done it all, and he's had a good deal of it done back to him. Death threats are a regular occurrence – but he's not about to let a little thing like that stop him doing his job.

'I have never been moved by threats,' he told us, leading the way through a series of locked gates and into the building. If the station looked run-down from the outside, things weren't much better inside. The walls had been half-heartedly painted in a shade of nicotine yellow – probably about 20 years ago – and were covered in a haphazard collage of noticeboards and 'wanted' posters. Rusty pipes banged and gurgled as we passed them. Desks were arranged randomly, overflowing with paper-work and files, and there always seemed to be about seven phones ringing at once. To be honest – and trust me, I'm not exactly fussy about these things – the whole place needed a good clean and tidy up. At the very least a lick of emulsion and a going over with a bucket and mop.

But still. Like they say, appearance isn't everything, a foul face can hide a fair heart and beauty is only skin deep. It didn't really matter what the place looked like, so long as it got the job done, right? As if to illustrate the point, Apollos eased himself into a chair behind the messiest desk of them all and resumed talking.

'I do receive death threats, but I've never been moved by them,' he repeated, 'regardless of what sort of threats have been issued to me or my family. I shouldn't be worried: it should be the other way round. The criminals should be worried that Apollos is on their trail.

'I am prepared to put my life on the line. I've come across a lot of dangerous situations and I haven't given up yet.'

Apollos leads the fight against organised crime from these unin-spiring surroundings. Boroko police station is where his team plan their raids on the country's criminal elite – and as it turned out, we'd arrived just in time to see them take down the biggest of them all.

✵   ✵   ✵

Papua New Guinea is located in the south-western Pacific Ocean, just to the north of Australia. It has a reputation as one of the most remote countries in the world, an idyllic wilderness unchanged for thousands of years, home to over 800 different traditional tribal societies speaking at least as many native languages … and, to be fair, all of that is true. The country is one of the least explored on the planet, both geographically and culturally, and the interior remains a mystery even to this day. Below the tranquil surface, however, lies a long history of tribal conflict and bloodshed.

And recently, this violence has moved from the isolated high-lands and jungles to the streets of the capital city, Port Moresby. Ancient grievances and cultural clashes that would once have been resolved with spears or bows and arrows are now settled at the point of a gun – often of the home-made variety.

Made with materials as crude as water piping and umbrella springs, these improvised firearms are nevertheless every bit as deadly as the real thing. And increasingly, as gun law takes hold of Port Moresby, the real thing is becoming easy to get hold of too.

Carjackings, shootouts and revenge killings keep the city in the grip of terror. With the situation at breaking point, a recent poll officially named Port Moresby as the worst city in the world. For this so-called paradise to be given that doubtful honour was an eye-opener, to say the least.

Battling to control the chaos are the Royal Papua New Guinea Constabulary. But the dramatic rise in violent crime here has not been matched by a rise in resources. In the shattered streets and shanty towns of Port Moresby, not only are the cops battling against high levels of lawlessness, but they're effectively having to do it with one arm tied behind their backs.

There are just 4,900 officers in the entire PNG force, policing a population of over six million people. With so few cops, catching criminals is an uphill battle.

The population of Port Moresby is just 300,000 – and the city is starkly divided. Decades of corruption in government has left some living the dream of the tropical paradise … but nearly half the population struggling to survive below the poverty line. The rich barricade themselves in mansions protected by razor wire; the rest make do in sprawling shanty towns, or 'settlements', creeping out like messy tentacles along the main roads leading in and out of the city.

Inhabited in large part by former tribesmen or farmers attracted to the city by a dream of streets paved with gold – or else forced to abandon generations-old family land by the ruthless march of capitalism – these slums have given rise to a new generation of criminal gangs. They call themselves the Raskols, and they're engaged in an all-out war with the police for control of Port Moresby's streets.

Thanks to an inherited culture of survival, strength and cunning passed on through thousands of years of tribal life, combined with a new viciousness and avarice learnt in the modern world, the Raskols are a threat like no other criminal gang in the world.

They have no pity, no mercy. We met one of them – and we were shocked by the casual nihilism he showed. Life is cheap to them, worthless even. They just don't care – about the police, about their victims, about anyone who gets in their way.

And as they've become more organised, they've grown in ambition too. It's no longer about carjackings and gang warfare: a recent spate of audacious heists has left the Port Moresby police in the grip of a new crisis.

❖   ❖   ❖

We had turned up on a big day for Port Moresby CID. Sergeant Apollos Terry was preparing to lead his men on a manhunt, and he was after the biggest criminal in the country, Papua New Guinea's most wanted man: one William Kapis.

In 2005 Kapis had escaped from jail – where he was serving a 22-year sentence for the attempted murder of a cop. The official line was that he had got out 'under the pretext of receiving medical attention' – but there were whispers of corruption, and insinuations (unproven) that he had inside help.

Whatever. Since his prison break Kapis hadn't exactly been lying low. He was the prime suspect in a series of major heists, including the robbery of cash worth three million PNG Kina (around $1 million) from several Bank South Pacific branches, as well as the theft of another million dollars' worth of gold bars. As if all that wasn't enough, he was also wanted for questioning over the murder of another policeman.

The operation had been months in the planning. His gang was known to number dozens – and rumoured to include several bent cops. Apollos simply could not afford to get such a high-profile bust wrong ... and if Kapis did indeed have men on the payroll of the Royal Papua New Guinea Constabulary then every detail of the take-down had to be classified top secret. Until the last minute only the most trusted members of his team even knew it was going to happen: and we, of course, were neither trusted nor members of his team.

We were not going on this raid.

As we met Apollos he was putting the final touches to the plan. They were going to raid the gang's hideout that evening – and they were expecting trouble. With Kapis already wanted for one cop killing, nobody was under any illusions as to his readiness to use guns in order to escape arrest.

'We've got the intelligence that they're armed,' Apollos told us, his face deadpan, as if he were remarking on nothing more serious than tomorrow's weather forecast. 'And we're expecting probably shootouts.' He shrugged. 'I think perhaps it's best you don't come with us.'

Dangerous it might have been, but the crew was gutted. This, after all, was what we were here for; and the chance to be a part of an operation to take down the country's most wanted man was just too good to let go that easily.

We tried appealing to Apollos's sense of investigative journalism. No good. We tried explaining how exciting it would look on TV. No good. We tried flattering him, cajoling with him, pleading, begging …

Apollos just smiled and shook his head. 'No,' he said, like a father gently but firmly telling his children it was time to go to bed. 'Not this time. Not on this trip. Maybe next time.'

We could only watch as the men were briefed – for most of the squad it was the first they knew about it, the security risk was classified that high – and then pulled on bullet-proof vests, checked and rechecked machine-guns, and loaded up into a convoy of 4x4 vehicles. We waved them out of Boroko police station. Some of them waved back, some just looked terrified. Apollos himself stuck his head out of the window and gave us the thumbs up. 'See you tomorrow,' he promised – and they were off, tyres squealing.

There was nothing left to do. We walked back through the gates and called it a night.

* * *

Bright and early just after dawn next morning and we were back in Boroko station car park. While we had been sleeping, Sergeant Apollos Terry and his team had been busy. They'd worked through the night and they were going to work through this day as well.

Apollos himself was taking a breather outside, sipping from a bottle of water, telling us how it had all gone down. He was wearing the same clothes as the night before – now spattered with blood. It wasn't his blood.

Although he looked knackered, he was every bit as calm as he had been the night before. Patiently, he explained what had happened.

First things first. They had got their man. His squad had ambushed three vehicles containing members of Kapis's gang (one of them a 10-seater landcruiser, another a bus) as they headed out of town, blocking them off from the front and rear and leaving them with no escape route.

The gang had not given up without a fight. Shots had been fired. Kapis himself was wounded in both legs ... but there were no police casualties. The dried sprays of blood decorating Apollos's shoes, trousers and shirt like the aftermath of an overshaken champagne bottle belonged to Papua New Guinea's most wanted man. And that man was now in a cell in this police station.

'OK then,' he said, taking a big pull of the bottled water. 'Basically what happened last night was that my men moved into the area where the gang were and we stopped them. We approached them in a very cautious way. He was considered dangerous. And armed as well. When we moved in he tried to escape. So we wounded him. He was taken to the hospital last night, treated, and he's now behind bars. I am pleased and at the same time I'm tired.'

Joining Kapis in these cells were 26 members of his gang. Three of them were serving cops. If it was a good result, the presence of the policemen amongst Kapis's gang made for a nasty sting in the tail. Once again, it raised unpleasant questions about the integrity of the Papua New Guinea force – and just how far Kapis's influence extended. How many more cops were on the payroll? If that was the first thing we wondered, you can bet your last PNG Kina that the same question was being asked at every level of the constabulary.

Kapis was clearly no ordinary prisoner, and so this place had become no ordinary police station. In the hours since his arrest Apollos hadn't been idle: Boroko station had been turned into a fortress. The place was locked down. The perimeter was guarded by cops with machine-guns on high alert for the first signs of trouble; we had needed Apollos himself to come out and authorise our entry past the guards at the front gate. Kapis had been busted out of jail once before: Apollos was dead set against it happening again.

'He has actually been caught on several occasions and locked up in cells,' he admitted, 'and he's managed to escape each time. So we're taking every precaution so that he doesn't escape again. We normally keep the most dangerous prisoner in a separate cell anyway.' He gestured towards a wing of the dilapidated building. 'That's the CID cell. So he's currently in one of those cells. Separate cells.'

We followed Apollos back into the station. He may have pulled an all-nighter but there was too much to do before he could even think about resting. When he did eventually get a chance to take a break it would be nothing more than a few hours' shut-eye in the station barracks. Apollos had already called his wife and told her not to expect him for a few days. It's a regular enough occurrence for her not to be too surprised.

'We normally work for eight-hour shifts,' he told us as we slowly made our way through a series of locked doors, past grim-faced cops with guns held ready. 'That's our normal hours and then we work extra hours depending on what needs to be done – maybe till around 11 or 12 o'clock in the night.' The tired-looking squad room was packed with cops; at every desk there was a man squinting at a computer screen and typing with one finger, or else frowning over sheaves of paper. More cops stood around in groups of twos and threes, shifting from foot to foot as if eager to get back out there. Apollos ignored them all and sank heavily into his own chair. 'Or sometimes, in a case of a wanted suspect like this, we'll work for up to two days non-stop,' he continued. 'Of course it's tiring, but once you get the results you want, then it all becomes worth it. And then you don't worry too much about the tiring part of it.'

The arrest of William Kapis was definitely the result the CID wanted. Not only had they successfully brought in Papua New Guinea's most wanted criminal without any officers getting injured, they'd nailed 26 of his gang at the same time.

'He was the most wanted man, so of course we are pleased,' he said, suddenly breaking into a grin, the deep-set, tired lines on his face all lifting at the same time. 'We are very happy that he's been busted and he won't cause any problems for anyone from now on. He should get 20, 25 years at least this time. Most of all it is a relief that such a man is off the streets now.'

So why was Apollos still here? He'd got his man, he'd pulled in a great result ... he should be at home sleeping the sleep of the just, right?

It wasn't that simple. Last night's raid was not the end of the story – they still had intel on several more of Kapis's gang that had not been amongst those arrested … and now that the word was on the street that the main man had been taken out, Apollos had to act fast before the remaining suspects got away.

The presence of the bent cops amongst the villains threw another spanner in the works. This operation was not finished yet – and while Apollos was acutely aware of that, he was also seriously frustrated at being stuck in this office instead of getting out and busting more bad guys.

What was the delay? Only the bane of every cop the world over. Paperwork.

'My men have to sit down and process documents for all the men who are currently in the cells,' he explained with a sigh. 'The cells are not even full yet, but basically all my detectives and officers are currently engaged in processing the necessary court papers. Hopefully they will appear in court probably tomorrow. And then once that is done and we've cleared these ones that we have already got … well, then we will conduct more police inquiries and probably more raids.'

We looked again around the room. If those concentrated frowns, the chewed pens, the one-fingered typing and the low hum of computer monitors all made sense now, then so did the body language of the other men in the room. Tired as they were, every one of these men was nonetheless desperate to get out of this crumbling station and back on to the streets.

Apollos smiled apologetically and opened his arms and huge hands wide, taking in the whole station. 'I do enjoy the action much better than paperwork,' he said, and laughed again.

These days, there's too much of both – and Apollos admits that he's pushing his men to the limit trying to stay on top of it all.

'Crime has dramatically changed from, I'd say, 2000 or so,' he said. 'Even up to 2005 you never heard about kidnappings, for example, but lately there's been a lot of robberies connected with kidnappings. They tend to kidnap important people in the family, like bank managers for example, and then order the bank manager to open the vault and get the loot. I think these new trends come from watching a lot of movies; they tend to adapt what they see from the movies.'

So was that was the key to the sudden explosion in crime here? Was the West to blame for introducing these ancient tribal cultures to a way of living where money and guns were shortcuts to power and status?

Money and guns. I've made a name for myself in the movies by playing hard men, ruthless men – and in those films I've handled a fair few weapons … and to be fair, it's given me a pretty comfortable lifestyle. Did that mean, in some weird, uncontrollable way, that I'd been part of what's turned this country into what it is today? It's a bit of a head-scrambler even thinking about it – not to mention a guilt trip.

Apollos just shrugged at that one. He was too savvy and had been in the force too long to get into questions like that. What he was prepared to say, however, was that the recent rise in crime had not been matched by a rise in resources for those men battling to keep the Raskols from ruining Port Moresby for ever.

'I cannot speak for other countries,' he said, 'but as far as Papua New Guinea goes, I think we simply lack the resources. So if the government pumped more money into the department, basically we would be able to control things better.' He gestured around the room, taking in the chronic state of the building he had to co-ordinate the fight from. 'I work in offices like this,' he said. 'We lack the resources. Like for example for this unit, they gave us just a couple of vehicles and then they wait and see what the results are. We've got good officers here, it's just that we need resources to back us up.

'I do think crime here is manageable; but what I'm saying is we want the government to invest more, give us what we need to do our jobs.'

For the moment, however, his underfunded, understaffed, under-resourced team were working like hell to try to stay on top of just this one operation. They were racing – against time and against logistics.

'If we do another raid, it will basically be more suspects in the cells,' he shrugged again. 'So we need to sort these ones out, get them out of the way and then we'll go to the next one.'

We wanted to know how long that would take – and, more to the point, if this time we would be able to tag along. After all, fascinating though all this was, we hadn't come all the way across the world to sit in a collapsing police station talking about crime fighting: we wanted to see it first hand.

Apollos smiled, like an indulgent father again. 'I promise that we'll go on a raid before you go,' he said. 'Tell you what. Come back this afternoon. We'll do one this afternoon. We'll do one especially for you.'

❋   ❋   ❋

Port Moresby CID may have taken out Papua New Guinea's most wanted man, but the cold hard truth was that removing William Kapis from the streets was just one small victory in a war that is going overwhelmingly against the forces of law and order here.

We'd heard about the Raskols, deadly criminal gangs who terrorise the community with daring robberies in broad daylight, armed hold-ups and brutal revenge killings. Descended from Papua New Guinea's ancient tribes, they've come from the lawless highlands to the city in search of a better life. And in Port Moresby, where, outside the fortified homes of the wealthy, half the population live in makeshift slums, they've created another kind of jungle. The Raskols control these settlements – many of them are often no-go areas, even for the police.

Their contempt for the law is so extreme that many of the Raskols view the police almost like their ancestors would see a rival tribe – with an open state of war declared, meaning that anyone in a uniform is a legitimate target. And should things get a little too hot, then they again do what their tribal ancestors would have done … and simply disappear into the highlands, the perfect hideout for criminals on the run from the cops.

It is the Raskols who are responsible for Papua New Guinea's explosion in violent crime – bringing a violent nihilism to the streets of this once peaceful country. It is the Raskols who are behind so many of the robberies, kidnappings and murders threatening to overwhelm the underfunded police force. And, with the help of a local fixer, it was the Raskols we were going to see in the hours before hooking back up with Apollos for the afternoon's raids. We had an appointment to meet up with a dangerous gang member deep inside their territory.

Our fixer drove us along streets that quickly disintegrated into muddy tracks, before pulling up in a makeshift car park behind a shack that served as a kind of café for the area. We were right on the edge of town; the houses were home-made – and while some seemed sturdy enough, others were ramshackle improvised hovels, barely having four walls and a roof. The highland jungles – visible from most of the city – seemed a little too close for comfort. We had to stop ourselves from imagining what might be lurking behind that dense, dark green wall of trees.

We'd hardly stopped when the passenger door opened and a hooded, bandana-wearing man stepped in. This was our Raskol.

He wouldn't tell us his name, and even through an interpreter his answers were short and to the point. Nonetheless, he painted a vivid enough picture of what drives young men like him to such extremes of lawlessness.

'We're called 007,' he said, before explaining that there were over 100 of them in his gang. The police estimate there to be at least 50 active Raskol gangs in Port Moresby – meaning there were probably around 5,000 dedicated violent criminals in this tiny capital alone.

'We do hold-ups and car thefts,' he went on. 'Sometimes we just stand by the road and if you're driving to the shops, or maybe back to your house, we just run after you and put a gun at your head, take you out of the car, get your car and go.'

And if somebody tries to resist?

'If you don't co-operate then we get to kill you. There'll be no warning shots. We're going to shoot you on the spot. We're after money, and if you disturb us or stop us getting the money than we'll kill you. It could be anybody. Men, women or children. Do I worry about killing another person? No I don't. How can I worry when there's plenty of people around?'

Raskol gangs are well armed, often with home-made guns. And with the criminals making their own weapons, it's impossible for the cops to control the number of guns on the street. We wanted to know if our man was carrying a weapon himself: underneath the bandana, we could sense a grin.

'Yeah. I do own a gun,' he said. 'It's a home-made gun. I've shot people, but I haven't killed anyone yet. Maybe I attempted to but I didn't successfully kill anyone yet.'

Not that he seemed too bothered about the idea. In settlements like these, there's little option but a life of crime, so there's no end to the violence in sight.

'If I did kill I wouldn't do it for fun, I'd do it for money,' he said. 'Who cares about the victim? Everyone's a victim. Everyone needs money to survive. If you don't have money you might as well kill another person to eat his flesh.'

What about the law? What about the cops?

'We have every right to shoot a policeman,' he said. 'Who cares? You shoot them, they shoot you. We are Papua New Guinean. We are meant to break the law.'

✿   ✿   ✿

Back in Port Moresby, Apollos was as good as his word. The CID were preparing to hit more members of Kapis's gang – and this time we were going along for the ride. Better than that: we were going to be right in amongst the action, riding shotgun with Apollos himself. He broke the news to us with that big fatherly smile … like it was Christmas and he was Santa Claus.

The mood in the station as the team of 10 were briefed was edgy, excited … but also shot through with nervousness. Those cops they had arrested the night before were still playing on some of the squad's minds. In a country as steeped in corruption as this, the only way the police can work effectively is for every man to have total trust and confidence in his comrades – once that bond goes, the criminals have already won half the battle.

The situation was so serious that Apollos's commanding officer had even been brought in to reassure his men. 'If you see any policemen acting suspiciously, get their names and report them to the superintendent,' he told the squad gravely. 'If any policeman steps out of line then I think there's no place in the police force for him – he's got to go. Let's work together, trust one another and move forwards, OK?'

The men nodded, fastened up their bullet-proof vests, shouldered their guns and got ready to roll. Despite the threats, there was work to be done.

They loaded themselves into 4x4s and hit the road, windows bristling with gun barrels. Thanks to the continuing paperwork situation, the team was bolstered by members of the elite mobile squad: everyone was packing enough heat to start a small war. No one was taking any chances.

Apollos, on the other hand, didn't carry a machine-gun. He trusted in his pistol – and, flouting every safety manual in the world, he drove his pick-up with gun drawn, somehow balancing it in his hand along with the gearstick.

'When we arrive at the location we will storm the house to surprise them,' he told us, flooring the gas again and shifting up, massive hands deftly juggling the gun and gears. 'That's the best ammunition for such operations.'

Behind us the rest of the team picked up their speed to match ours, and together the squad raced through the streets towards one of the city's poorer settlements. 'We have intelligence reports that there is actually ammunition and firearms in the location,' he continued. 'So if we do come across anyone with a firearm we're ready for anything. They're not expecting us now, so I don't think they'll be rolling out the red carpet ...'

After 20 minutes' drive – and at a legal speed it would have taken twice as long as Apollos took – we screamed into the targeted neighbourhood. We couldn't help feeling relieved to see it was not the same one we had visited earlier.

Apollos flashed his indicators and behind him everyone cruised to a stop. The house directly in front of us stood out from all the others around. This was no shanty shack: iron gates at least seven feet high barred the driveway; the building beyond was large, spacious – it even included a double garage. Apollos surveyed the scene for a moment, slowly taking it all in: we could almost hear his brain ticking over. He frowned, and then ordered us out of the car.

The gates were going to have to be dealt with, one way or another. And when it comes to making an entrance, Apollos Terry doesn't mess about.

We'd barely shut the doors behind us when he revved the 4x4 until it screamed, before releasing the brake and crashing straight into the barriers. They buckled, the lock smashed, and he was in. Within seconds the whole team were in there with him, and the big man led the charge.

Crash! The front door was kicked in with one weighty swing of his right foot, and clutching his small pistol Apollos charged through the house. Behind him came the men with machine-guns, like troops in the trenches following their sergeant over the top.

It only took a minute to secure the house. The gang weren't here – Apollos reckoned they'd been tipped off after the previous raids. But the good news was they'd left in a hurry. 'I think they were here last night,' he nodded, gesturing around the house. It didn't even look like they'd taken any clothes with them. 'We're looking for firearms or money that was stolen during the robberies,' he continued, as the squad fanned out through the house and began methodically searching the place.

It wasn't long before they made a shocking discovery. Brand new military uniforms, freshly pressed. This find could be a vital piece of evidence to help convict Kapis and his gang of some of Papua New Guinea's most high-profile robberies. It's not as if these uniforms can be picked up down at the local army surplus store either – in this country it's an offence for a civilian to be in possession of such official uniforms. We asked how they might have come by them.

'Well, probably from the army,' he said, raising his eyebrows. It was, on reflection, a bit of a stupid question. Shaking his head, he continued: 'They're probably from their guys, their friends in the military. So it is probably some kind of inside help. But we'll check with the owner of the house when we find him. But definitely he will be charged with those uniforms.

'We've had instances where major robberies are committed using military and police uniforms.'

The clothes were bagged up and taken out to one of the pick-ups as evidence. As we watched, other cops started to systematically dismantle the house. In the garage were a stack of vehicle licence plates – including a 'Z' plate, reserved for government use. Was it stolen from an official car? Or was it a fake to be used in a future robbery? Apollos was uneasy about it – but certain that the raid was a result.

'Look around,' he said. 'For a vagrant he's doing fine, isn't he? He's got a 4x4 and a small car. He's living in a good house …' and it was a house filled with all mod cons. As we stood watching, however, most of those mod cons were taken out and loaded into the jeeps. Two men lugged out what looked like a brand-new aircon unit, while another had an enormous keyboard, and behind him a cop carried out a state-of-the-art fax machine. Any one of these items would have cost more than most Port Moresby ghetto-dwellers could hope to make in a year.

Following them back out into the driveway and nodding his approval, Apollos continued: 'Somebody who's not working, unemployed, you know? You can't expect these things to be in the house. We believe that he could have been involved with these guys one way or the other. What we do now is we take all this to the station, we lock them up and it's for him to come and explain where he got these things from, where he got the money to buy them. We also found some police uniforms and army shirts. During the robberies, they were using police uniforms and pretending to be a policeman ...' He stopped by his car and patted the bonnet. 'So when he comes we will be definitely laying some charges against him anyway.'

It was time to get on to the next location. 'Let's start moving things before they start phoning each other,' he shouted, and the men doubled the pace. Within minutes they were done, and most of the shinier, more expensive contents of the house were on their way to the station. Apollos jumped back into the 4x4. 'We're going to a place called Rainbow,' he said, as the convoy took off again. 'That's our next target. They're believed to be William Kapis's accomplices. Such missions are always dangerous.'

Thankfully, when we got to the second location we still held the element of surprise. A group of eight suspected gang members were lazing in the garden – we were on top of them before they had time to react: and with gun barrels in their faces and the heavy bulk of Apollos Terry bearing down on them, they didn't have much choice but to stay calm and play nice.

We stood with them as Apollos's men searched the property. They came back with a stash of ammunition.

Time for a little gentle interrogation, Apollos Terry style. 'Listen,' he said, talking quietly, all reasonable, the concerned father figure again. 'We don't want to go to the extreme of getting fingerprints on these. Do you understand? Just tell us and we will leave. Do you understand? Will you own up?'

Unsurprisingly, none of the gang admitted to anything. So Apollos got tough. Leaning in dangerously close to the men's faces, he spat his words out, still quiet but now filled with terrible menace. This wasn't Santa Claus any more – this was an aspect of the big cop we hadn't been exposed to. And we sure as hell didn't want to be on the wrong side of it.

'Listen,' he said, and as he talked the men visibly paled before him. 'If you know whose they are just say or else you'll be injured. You people better start talking. Start talking and you won't feel the pain.'

There was a moment of perfect silence. And then the moment stretched … and stretched. We couldn't believe it: the men stayed shtum. I have to wonder whether if I'd been in the same position I would have sung like a canary.

Apollos eyed them furiously, the way a boxer eyes his opponent the moment before the bell goes for the start of Round One … and then sighed and turned away. Behind him, the men were cuffed and squeezed into a van, to be taken back to the station for more questioning. They were shaking with fear.

'We found bullets,' he said to us. 'We will take them to the police station and ask them where the firearm is.'

We asked if they were all under arrest.

'Yes,' he sighed. 'Yes, they're under arrest.'

* * *

We'd finally seen Papua New Guinea's most respected, most feared cop in action – and while not so obviously flashy as some of the officers we'd met around the world, his total sense of authority was overwhelming. Twenty-three years on the force has given him that: it was only ever going to be Apollos Terry who would smash in the gates to a suspect's house; it was only ever going to be Apollos Terry who would lead his men into a potential shootout with just a pistol against machine-guns ... and it was only ever going to be Apollos Terry who would terrify a gang of suspects the way we had just seen him do.

He was like one of those teachers you had at school that you were half in awe of, half terrified of. The sort you wanted to impress because you wanted him to like you ... but also because you were seriously worried about what might happen if he decided he didn't like you.

No wonder he has such a reputation here. He shrugs off death threats, and accepts the almost total devotion of his men in the same way that a father knows he can count on the loyalty of his children. And with that in mind, there was one thing left to do with Apollos to get to the very heart of what makes him tick. We wanted to meet his family.

We didn't really expect him to be up for the idea (given those death threats and all), but when we put it to him he just gave the old shrug and smiled as if to say, sure, why not? Half an hour later he was driving us out of the city.

If we were surprised at where we were headed, we tried not to show it. But somehow, we didn't expect Sergeant Apollos Terry to live in one of Port Moresby's 'settlements' – the polite name for the kind of near shanty towns we'd seen too much of on this trip already.

'Where I live ... well it is a settlement,' he explained. 'A settlement is a government land and then people migrate from other places, they come and just ... build a house – and they are all unplanned, so basically it's a community of unplanned building popping up anywhere.'

This, presumably, was one of the more respectable settlements, however? Well, no.

'It is a notorious settlement,' he continued, nodding his head for emphasis. 'Criminal activities … there's a lot of activities down where I live. But then I actually grew up there, so maybe for me it's much safer. And now, being a policeman myself, the community are very pleased and happy that I am living amongst them so when they have problems in their house, they normally run across to my house and I help them sort out these matters.'

As we were about to find out, however, it wasn't really that simple. For Apollos's wife and three children, having such a high-profile cop as head of the house didn't always mean the respect and admiration of the local community.

❊　　❊　　❊

The house itself was no shack – but it was not in the same league as either of the properties we had busted earlier in the day. A simple, functional, scrupulously clean place, it was filled with the knick-knacks and mementoes of family life. It could have been a family home anywhere – were it not for the subtle, telltale signs that things here aren't quite so straightforward.

On one of the walls was a handwritten notice, headed 'House rules'. And after rule number 1 it started to get a little ominous: '1. No absence from school. 2. No visitors. No sleepovers. 3. No games. 4. Vehicle only for school runs. 5. Driver either Paps or Helen's Hubby.' We didn't know who Helen's Hubby was, but we guessed he was connected to the force somehow. Either way, it seemed the kids didn't exactly live a carefree life here in the settlement.

As we entered, Apollos's wife Kivea met us with a shy smile. Dressed in blue vest and black trousers, she looked tiny beside the imposing bulk of her husband, but nonetheless held herself with a calm self-assurance. She explained how she too has seen this country descend into Raskol-led chaos.

'I'm from the highlands,' she told us, 'but I've been raised in Port Moresby all my life. But in those days before, maybe 10 years ago, maybe 20 years ago, you felt a sense of security, you could walk around. There was respect for others. But these days you have a sense of fear. That anybody would come and, you know, mug you. You don't have that feeling of security any more.

'Like for me and my kids, we can't go out as much as we would like to, and when we do go out, we always make sure we have someone with us. We don't allow the kids to go out on their own. There's always somebody chaperoning them. All basically because of that fear and because of his line of work.'

As we had begun to suspect, it seemed that Apollos's reputation on Papua New Guinea wasn't all positive. And where his family were concerned, it meant living in constant fear of the consequences of his work. So much so that Kivea and the kids don't even share his name, just in case the wrong person makes the connection.

'It's because of his line of work that me and my children use a different surname from him,' she told us. 'That's one of the precautions we take. And most of the time we are not seen with him. Especially when he's out at work. We leave him to do his stuff and then he comes home to us. That's what we do.

'A lot of times in the past there have been death threats issued against him. And when he does get those threats he immediately lets me know, and then I quickly let the children know, and we explain to them that this and that has happened and, y'know, these kinds of threats are coming. And we have to be very cautious about how we move, especially out in the public. Sometimes, it gets frustrating, sure. But then, we have respect for his work, and so we just take it. And just hope that nothing happens.'

And then perhaps the strangest thing of all happened. Apollos's children were ushered into the room, standing politely with arms folded behind the sofa on which he and Kivea sat. They were two girls of about 12 and 14 (at a guess – nobody seemed very forth-coming with their names or ages) and the eldest, David, who had just turned 17. All were tall, athletic, good-looking kids … and they were clearly on their best behaviour.

'Obviously we're really proud of him,' said the oldest daughter, staring straight down at us with a defiant look in her eye. 'He's a nice dad. He always thinks of us. Puts us first in everything he does.'

Her younger sister nodded vigorously. 'You're seeing that my dad's awesome in his work and is the best dad,' she declared. 'We, uh, we sometimes get annoyed with our parents for keeping us in the house all the time, but we're used to it so now we enjoy being by ourselves.'

There was a moment of silence. And what about David, the young man of the family, Apollos Terry's son and heir?

'Uh … I get worried,' he said, staring at the floor and stammer-ing slightly. 'But uh – I – I – don't usually … they see that I'm OK, then they'll feel all right, yeah? And, um – we get threats from people. And stuff. We get scared, y'know? And we don't go out much. We don't socialise with the uh, the other children.'

Apollos leaned over and ruffled his hair, before turning back to us and giving that wide, enveloping smile again. It was our cue to leave. On the way out we passed another sign, this one nailed above the doorway.

'God Bless Our Home,' it said.

SHERIFF FATMAN:
A DAY IN THE LIFE OF BIGGA FORD

Cornwall 'Bigga' Ford. It doesn't sound like a cop's name. And the man himself doesn't look too much like the Old Bill either. Not for nothing is he called Bigga – he's massive, a mountain, 20 stone at least. And he's even been known to wear his hair in dreads.

But then this is Jamaica. Everything's a little bit different here. And make no mistake: in Jamaica, Bigga Ford is the man.

Bigga heads up the Jamaican Flying Squad – what in Britain we used to call The Sweeney. But that's where the similarity ends: this guy could eat Regan and Carter for breakfast. Almost literally.

He's a bit of a legend on the island, is Bigga. A cop since 1976, he's grown in both stature and reputation since then – and now his no-nonsense, firm-but-fair approach, plus a healthy streak of eccentricity, has made him one of the best-known men in the Caribbean. He's a regular source of headlines for the newspapers here, and he's name-checked in the lyrics of some of the biggest reggae, ragga and dancehall hits. But most important of all, he's got the ear of the local communities.

Oh – and he also boasts a clear-up rate that's nothing short of astonishing.

On the mean streets of Kingston, where it matters most, Bigga Ford is hailed as a hero.

'When the place is mashed up, only he can cool it; only he can bring it back,' says one lady from the notorious Constant Spring area. 'Bigga Ford is a hero everywhere he goes. He knows how to deal with the citizens the right way. He knows everybody, he knows the right and the wrong.'

We spent an average working day on the beat with Bigga: a day that just happened to begin with a cop killing.

❉   ❉   ❉

KINGSTON, JAMAICA. EIGHT A.M. and a small white car weaved and hustled its way through the rush-hour traffic.

On any Monday morning the streets are choked with cars, but this was the first day back at work after the Caribbean Easter break and the city was gridlocked.

Superintendent Cornwall 'Bigga' Ford was in no mood to hang around, however. His massive bulk filling the unmarked car, he threw the steering wheel around with one hand, slamming the horn with the heel of his palm, hollering out of the window for people to get out of his way.

His voice – somewhere between typical lilting Caribbean patois and the bellow of a bull elephant – cut through the bedlam in the streets. 'Whatcha doin' wit de bus? Get outta mi way, man! Hey! Outta mi way wit de bus!'

Somehow, as if by the sheer physical force of the man himself, he manoeuvred the vehicle around the traffic, shouldering his way through the jumble of cars and lorries, buses and bikes, mopeds and taxis.

It's the start of another week for Bigga – and it couldn't have begun worse.

The night before had seen yet another shooting – not such an unusual occurrence in this city, where easy access to guns and drugs have ramped up simmering gang tensions into something way more deadly. But that morning things had got far messier. Word had got out, and the dead man's crew had come looking for vengeance. As the rest of Kingston was waking up, having breakfast, getting ready for work, out on the streets up to six gunmen had clashed. Worse: a police officer had got caught up in the crossfire.

'What is actually happening is there is some shooting up in the Constant Spring area,' explained Ford to us, squeezed into the car alongside him. 'From information coming to us, one man has been shot and killed. Another person has been injured and a police officer was also shot and injured. The Flying Squad team, we're going up to give our assistance right now.'

Police were already on the scene, but with anything up to four of the shooters still at large Bigga and his boys were battling to reach them before further damage could be done.

'This is dangerous, you know?' he warned us. 'Very, very dangerous and rough. My team, the men are in armoured gear. We are using the M16 rifles and stuff, we go prepared. When an officer is down it's almost like I'm down also.'

'Frank! Frank!' he yelled, one arm waving out of his window at the car behind, 'Tek a right, man! Tek a right!'

Finally, the cars broke free of the main streets and Bigga floored the accelerator. As the roads deteriorated into little more than dusty tracks, and the smarter shops, high-rises and restaurants gave way to shabbier stores, lopsided shacks and dirty concrete houses, the car bounced crazily and we were thrown around, barely able to keep ourselves in our seats.

Only Bigga Ford remained immovable. Letting go of the steering wheel completely for a moment as his radio squealed and crackled, he picked it up. 'Yeah man, go 'head, go 'head. All right, we are in the Cassava Piece area.'

Up ahead a crowd had gathered and Ford finally brought his car to a skidding stop. As he eased himself out and dusted himself off, our director almost dropped his camera as we were greeted with the strangest sight we'd come across in all our travels.

Right here, in one of the city's poorest ghettoes, where talking to the wrong people can be fatal, the kind of place where the tourists don't go and the police travel in packs, the arrival of the superintendent was treated like the appearance of a superhero – as if Bruce Willis himself had showed up to sort it all out.

If this had been a scene in one of my movies, I'd have wanted a chat with the director. These things just don't happen in real life. No one watching the film would believe it.

But it was happening here all right.

The crowd erupted into spontaneous cheering. 'Bigga! Bigga!' they cried, women in sandals and T-shirts launching into impromptu shuffling dances, old men with grizzly beards grinning, boys in vests and bare feet clapping along. 'Bigga here! When the place is mashed up he can bring it back!'

Behind them, in the middle of the dusty street, lay the body of a man. He was sprawled face down, with his arms and legs at crazy angles and a shoe half off one foot. Perfectly still. Flies already buzzing around his head.

Bigga waved the cheering crowds away and heaved his way through them towards the corpse. He chatted quietly with one of the six or seven policemen standing awkwardly around the body: his suit trousers and immaculately ironed, pure white shirt (buttoned up despite the heat) in stark contrast to their body armour, combat trousers, boots and M16 rifles. Nodding slowly, he spoke into his radio again and beckoned us over, out of earshot of the crowds.

'Well, what we are seeing now is a police fatal shooting,' he said. 'Information coming to me is that there was a shooting on Mannings Hill Road earlier last night where a man was shot and killed. The police were in pursuit of some people this morning and during that shootout this man was shot and killed. And the police officer was also shot and killed.'

Cornwall Bigga Ford's week was barely an hour old and he already had three murders, one of them a fellow cop, to deal with.

JAMAICA

'It's too hot,' he sighed. 'We got a lot of problems.'

＊　　＊　　＊

Jamaica is an island with a lot of problems of its own. Far from being the tropical paradise of popular culture, all palm trees and cricket and sparkling sandy beaches, the reality is that Kingston is one of the most violent cities on the planet. The sun, sea, reggae, rastas and ganja are all real enough – but there's a flipside too.

Jamaica has one of the highest murder rates in the world – with an average of at least one killing every nine hours and more than four a day. We were there in 2008: and of the 1500 gun-related killings in the year before we arrived, 19 of the victims were cops shot down and murdered in the line of duty. That's more than one every three weeks. Only six days passed in all of 2007 in which no Jamaican was reported murdered.

That same year there were 82 double murders, 10 triple murders and five quadruple murders. And in case you're not sure exactly what a quadruple murder is … it's a bloodbath.

In 2006, the year before, 65 of the victims were children.

And, as with most of the places we visited, the worst of the problems get concentrated into the big city. Jamaica does have its idyllic beaches, its tourist havens, its pockets of Caribbean heaven … but not so many of them in Kingston town.

With a population of just 650,000, Kingston is Jamaica's capital – but thanks to gangs, guns and drugs, it has also become known as one of the world's murder capitals.

The drugs arrive from Colombia, transported in thousands of ships that slip in along the 146 miles of coastline and offload before the police can catch up with them. The smugglers are not only fuelling a local narcotics economy but also using the island as a stepping-stone to the big markets in America and Europe. According to the United Nations, 10 tonnes of cocaine come through here every year – which makes the 260 kilos the cops have seized in the last two years seem pretty tame in comparison.

And it's not just drugs that find their way on to the island. Every year hundreds of illegal guns pitch up in Jamaica. Where do they come from? Colombia? America? Who knows. The cops don't – and they can't stop them coming. In 2007 the police seized 630 guns – but it was a drop in the ocean, a gesture as much as anything. As the murder statistics show in the starkest black and white, the weapons are still arriving somehow, still finding their way into the hands of the bad guys.

It's all made murder an everyday occurrence here – worse even: it's made murder a four-times-a-day habit. Think of it as breakfast, lunch, dinner and a snack before bed. In Jamaica people are killed more often than they eat.

We had come to find out what makes a cop in this place. Why do the job in a city so dangerous that 19 of your fellow officers can get gunned down in a single year? It's not the money: the basic annual salary is only around two and a half thousand pounds.

Nevertheless, the 7,000 members of the Jamaica Constabulary Force in Kingston do their very best to police this capital city against a rising tide of violence – and they do it despite knowing that it's one of the most dangerous jobs in the world.

With the murder stats at such a level, the sheer volume of death can seem unmanageable for the cops, with an endless line of faceless victims and a population scared of giving up the kind of information that might lead to convictions. And of course the problem is not just a matter of how to solve the crimes: it's surviving long enough to do it. The terrible reality for the men and women on the front line is that getting up and going to work each day can literally be a matter of life and death.

So here we were, in Kingston, Jamaica, looking for the world's toughest cops. But where to start?

✻   ✻   ✻

Our contacts had set us up with a number of different Jamaican police agencies. We went out with the Marine Patrol – a unit charged with the task of preventing drugs from entering the island. Operating a fleet of just 12 high-powered boats and up against the full force of the South American cartels, they're hopelessly outnumbered ... but we sailed with them as they intercepted some of the hundreds of fishing boats used to transport the contraband.

These guys aren't your average coastguards; they come seriously tooled up. As Sergeant Everton Reynolds explained: 'If we have to use force we will use as much force as is necessary. Sometimes we are warned that these people are heavily armed. So we carry M16 rifles and Glock pistols as sidearms. If we should encounter these guys out there, then it's either we protect ourselves or they get the better of us.

'They're always trying to stay one step ahead of us and we are always trying to stay one step ahead of them. It's an ongoing war ...'

We then rolled with patrol officers Corporal Byron Lewis and his partner in the Mobile Patrol Unit as they hit a 14-hour night shift on the streets of Kingston. It didn't take long before they got word of a shooting – and we were with them as they edged, lights out and guns at the ready, into Rockfort, a notorious part of Kingston's East Side, in pursuit. That time things were just too risky for two patrol cops on their own – Lewis called in the Jamaican army as back-up and we got the hell out.

'There is a thin line between a fool and bravery,' explained Corporal Lewis. 'It's a thin line and a lot of people can't distinguish which is which. So if shots are raining down and you want to walk out in it, I wouldn't say its bravery – that's stupidity.

'When you look at the type of armour that these guys have, you have few numbers and they have real powerful weapons. You have to wonder and think back, where do these weapons come from? How do these weapons end up in the hands of a teenager? How, by what means?'

His partner chipped in: 'They can't afford to buy food, they are barefoot, without a shirt, and torn clothes. At the same time they have rifles valued at 300,000 Jamaican dollars.'

'Exactly,' continued Lewis. 'So how does a weapon of that magnitude reach into the hands of criminals?'

They couldn't give us an answer.

We met Detective Pat Crosby of the Murder Investigation Unit – a man who admits his shifts are not a question of *if* he'll be called to a murder scene, but how many times he will.

'These guys are not firing any small-calibre weapons, they are firing high-powered weapons so they can stay at a far distance to fire on you,' he told us. 'So it's very difficult when you have to attend a crime scene here, or respond to any shootings. Very difficult. But it takes good hearts, strong will, to really continue doing the job.

'Going to crime scenes, for me, in my 21 years' service in this work, has not gotten any easier on the mind. It may have got easier on the eyes, because I've gotten used to seeing it so much, but mentally it's not good. It keeps going around in my head: why does this continue to happen?'

Crosby admits that at times the sheer scale of the problem can make trying to combat the murders seem like a hopeless task. And he's worried that the citizens of Kingston themselves – even the law-abiding people he's trying to protect – are growing numb to the horror of it.

'It can be, oh another man has died, oh it happened yesterday and the day before,' he said. 'It's just another part of life. They become so used to seeing these things it's like nothing no more. Just like that.'

But time after time, these officers, these front-line men holding the thin blue line between order and chaos on the streets of Kingston, would ask us the same questions: have we met the Flying Squad? Have we talked to Bigga Ford?

In this dangerous city, when the public are in trouble they call in the police. But when the police are in trouble they call in the Flying Squad – the Jamaica Constabulary Force's elite unit.

And nothing says trouble like a cop killing. The death of a cop does something to policemen. Any officer investigating a murder wants to see the killer brought to justice – it's what they do, it's why they do it. But when one of their own is slain … it matters more. It becomes personal. If the Jamaican gangs have a culture of reprisal killings, then the same burning thirst for revenge consumes every cop who sees a comrade killed in the line of duty.

Here in Kingston, you don't have to search too hard to find a cop who's walked that line. As Corporal Lewis of the Mobile Patrol Unit told us: 'I lost a close, close colleague of mine just two weeks ago. He took a taxi, and they were robbing the taxi, and someone recognised or realised that he was a police officer and they held him up and shot him twice and dumped his body on the roadway. It's really hard to know that someone was this close and you have lost them to some violent attack.

'It makes me feel very bad, honestly. It's a bit discouraging, but, guess what, if everyone should drop their arms as a result of what is happening, we would not have a force to fight anything and crime would go on a rampage. So somebody has to do it, you understand?'

People on either side feel angry when someone they know is killed, but the big difference is that those on the right side of the law keep their vengeance legal. Just don't think for a second that their anger doesn't burn so bright.

We made the call. And at 7 a.m. on the Monday after the Easter break, we met Superintendent Cornwall Bigga Ford. Less than an hour later we were hurtling through the gridlocked streets with the man on the way to the scene of a cop killing.

* * *

So there we were. And in that dusty street in Constant Spring, with one body sprawled in the dirt in front of him, another shooter in the hospital and a cop on his way to the morgue, Superintendent Cornwall Bigga Ford wasn't in the mood to mess around.

'When an officer is down it's almost like I'm down also,' he said. 'When a police officer is killed the high command mobilise all resources available in order to make an arrest as soon as possible. So it can bring closure, but also to bring back confidence to the officers working on the street – and to the public at large.

'I'm like a father figure to the team. I try to operate this unit in a family setting. I'm the superintendent, it's automatic that I take the role as protector of my staff. Any loss will greatly affect the whole unit, all of us.'

But right then it was first things first. The crowd – who minutes before had been hailing the arrival of Bigga Ford like a saviour –

were beginning to get restless again, and the rank-and-file police officers guarding the scene looked edgy too.

It was time to roll. Leaving the cops on the scene to mop up, Bigga hit the road. If he was on the hunt for a cop killer, he was going to do it the old-fashioned way. Intel. Info. Gather the word on the street.

Back in the car, Bigga was taking it easy, sparing the accelerator. This time it was strictly cruise control, idling along the jumbled, chaotic streets around Constant Spring and the Mannings Hill Road areas. The window wound down, one enormous arm hanging out of the car, his eyes constantly scanning the crowds. Every minute or so he leant what he could of his massive bulk out of the window. 'Hey! Did you see the shoot-up? Wha' 'appen here? Everyting a'right? I hear they're mashin' up your area?'

Unbelievably, people stopped to talk.

Two men in vests and dreads sauntered over, exchanging lazily complicated handshakes, drawling in heavy patois, shrugging shoulders, shaking heads. Another guy with yellowed eyes and pockmarked skin whispered in his ear, leaning into the car, filling the vehicle with the heady, sweet smell of the street. Three ladies in the market district shouted over to us as we cruised past – 'Yo, Bigga! What up?'

The super idled the car and shouted back. 'You know police are dead? You know another man died last night? A man died again today. And I told you the boy was going to mash up the place. We'll deal with it. Me personally, I will deal with it, all right?'

Another lady insisted he get out of the car and talk away from us. As we watched she spoke rapidly, urgently, into his ear; they separated with a hug before she hurried on. Each time he left the car, the doors remained unlocked, the engine running. Bigga himself made no attempt to hide the pistol stuck into his trouser belt – and even when he was pushing his way through the hustle and bustle of downtown Kingston, squeezing his way through the crowds of people, he showed not the slightest concern that some-one might try to snatch his weapon, or that the car might get nicked. Why? Partly maybe a typically Caribbean laid-back atti-tude on his part … and partly respect on everyone else's. Only a fool would try to steal Bigga Ford's wheels. And you'd have to be suicidal to even think about lifting the gun.

Within minutes of starting the intel run, the information began to come in and Bigga's phones started ringing. The only phones that mattered right then were in his enormous shirt pocket: two of them, to be precise, one for each mobile network. He wants to make sure that it's as easy – and cheap – for people to reach him as possible … and it's the kind of smart touch that has made him such an effective policeman.

His mobiles have different ringtones: each of them an ear-split-ting, distorted mp3 of some frenetic dancehall tune. They never rang long enough for us to hear anything past the first couple of bars – and his conversations were just as rapid, Bigga doing all the listening, never writing anything down, filing it all away in his head.

'Even though they speak to me, they're afraid,' he explained. 'Because when the people who commit these crimes see them speaking to me, they automatically assume they're passing on information, and they're branded informers. So a lot of people generally take my telephone numbers and give me a call. And I listen. Anybody can speak to me. Everyone knows I don't have a problem with that.

'My philosophy's very simple,' he continued. 'If you do your work and live good with the people, the people will trust you. And once the people trust you, they'll speak to you. I try to do my best.

'If you're a street cop the people will deal with you, will trust you, will respect you and have confidence in you. It's all on the level. You need to have the people on the road who intertwine with the general populace. And if they feel you have the integrity they will speak to you and they'll tell you a lot of things.'

It's a two-way street, of course. The tips and titbits Bigga was collecting come at a price, one way or another.

'Policing is a work where you have to be all things to all persons,' he said. 'You have to be the police officer, you have to be the teacher, the doctor, the social worker ... you have to work all things. The people in the community have different needs. So some people come to me and say Ford, can you help me get my son or daughter in school? You have to try and assist. Some people say they can't afford to send their kids to school today, you have to give a little lunch money. Some say their child needs to go to a doctor and they can't afford a doctor fee. So you know a doctor that you can make a contact with and will give up his service for free ... stuff like that, you know?

'Policing in Jamaica means being a person who does everything for everybody. You have to go to funerals, weddings, graduation – they invite you to anything. And that's the way it works if we want the citizens to come on board and tell us what they need.'

Two calls came in that morning that especially interested him. One from a guy who had seen us cruising – he had a couple of candidates; the other from the injured gunman, phoning from his hospital bed. He wanted to give up some names too.

It was time to get back to headquarters.

✼　　✼　　✼

Bigga was under no illusions as to what sparked the killings. Rival gangs have turned parts of Kingston into hostile war zones: there are an estimated 32,500 gang members in this city – that's five per cent of the entire population – and they outnumber the cops by four to one.

Gang crime in Kingston has a long and violent history dating back more than 40 years to 1962, when Jamaica gained independence from Great Britain. The two main political parties – the People's National Party (PNP) and the Jamaica Labour Party (JLP) – vied for control of the island: gangs were formed with allegiances to these parties and territorial lines were drawn. More than 40 years later they are still at war.

However, the roots of organised violence in Jamaica can be traced back further still, to the late 1940s and the heated political battles between the founders of the two parties. Even back then, tough inner-city neighbourhoods were divided according to PNP and JLP loyalties, with party supporters choosing to live together in certain areas and rival party supporters forced out.

By the 1970s and 80s, the relationship had developed into something far more organised – and more sinister: the shadier politicians and the gang leaders had become mutually dependent on one another. The gang leaders – also called 'dons' – ensured party loyalty in their areas, delivering votes where it mattered and intimidating rival supporters into staying away from the ballot boxes ... and the politicians repaid them with public works programmes and public housing.

But then something shifted. Politics was cleaned up to some extent ... but on the streets, far more importantly, drugs and guns changed the game for ever. Although party loyalties still broadly divide the neighbourhoods, these days the gangs are into far more lucrative ventures. Dealing, smuggling, protection, extortion.

These have given the gangs a newfound control over whole communities that owes little to those in power. 'Community justice' – another name for self-ruling kangaroo courts – are common, as the gangs dispense with the police and politicians altogether. A recent investigation by a children's charity into Jamaica's gang warfare concluded: 'Residents don't have much faith in the justice system, and turn to the gangs or dons for justice. One young man said that "people gettin' beatings for rape [and] thievery from gangsters, corner gangs [and] guys who are runnin' the place. They don't want a thief or rapist in the community." A group of youth from August Town said punishments for such offences could include beatings and torture by electric shock.'

It's a mess. Kingston newspaper *The Gleaner* summed it up best: 'The deadly alliance formed between politicians from the two major political parties and criminals has destabilised the country to the extent that politicians are now powerless in the dangerous game they foisted on society.'

This is what Bigga and his men have to deal with. This is their mess to clean up. But, typically of the man, he's sticking by his principles: get out on the street, build confidence from the bottom. Play fair, give respect, get respect.

✾   ✾   ✾

The pieces were falling into place. Bigga had a picture of what had gone down. The night before, it seemed, a long-running dispute between two local gangs had flashed up into violence: leaving one man dead. Word had got out overnight, and early in the morning the brothers of the dead man had gone out looking for revenge. They found the shooters at about the same time as the cops, and in the resulting three-way gunfight, one of the policemen was downed ... along with the victim we had seen, still lying face down in the street. A third man had been injured: the cops had got him out of there and to hospital.

What had been unclear was who exactly was involved – and what sides the dead men had been on. But now, thanks to an hour or two cruising the streets, names were being put to faces ... and a plan was being formed.

On the way to the station he explained a little of what made him tick. 'I don't have a no-go area in Jamaica,' he said. 'I'll go to the football, the dancehall, I'll go anywhere. I don't have a problem. If the need arises and I have to go, I'll go, and I'll go alone. Some people recognise me but I don't have a problem. If you treat people justly and fairly the people will look after you and protect you. I'm not saying I'm a hero, and I don't want to be a martyr. You just have to develop that confidence and trust.'

Bigga started his career back in 1976, pounding the beat – albeit slowly, he was a big man even then – and within four years had made acting corporal. A series of rapid promotions followed, culminating with his being made a detective in the CID, and appointed inspector in 1991. But two years later, the police commissioner put him back in uniform and back on the streets, assigned to the Stony Hill area.

Rather than be disheartened, however, Bigga just did what he does best. Crime in Stony Hill fell away to near zero under his watch – and in 1999 he was promoted back into the Flying Squad. Three years later he took charge of Kingston's most elite police unit.

'The unit I command is the Flying Squad,' he explained. 'It's comprised of about 60 specialist detectives. We only accept specialists. They are multi-faceted, and they're all trained by the FBI and the UK police. They can investigate crimes from simple reports to major cases of murder. We are an operational arm of the Criminal Investigation Branch, but we're also investigators as well as being a tactical unit. And we're equipped so that we can take on any situation.

'We're a tough unit. We're the Flying Squad; sometimes we do fly. If we're in the office and there's a shooting and our assistance is required, we'll put on the armour, get the M16s and go assist. The situation has to be bad for the Flying Squad to be called in.

'The criminal community fear us. The underworld has respect for my squad, because once we commence the operation, we'll see it through. Our success rate is almost 95 per cent. We'll do our job until we see that person before a court.'

Part of Bigga's reputation on this island comes from his total willingness to get in there when it matters – along with his complete lack of fear. In 2006 he nearly paid for it with his life.

'The people know me but the criminals know me also,' he said. 'Some are scared of me, some aren't. I've been shot at, shot and injured. You have to understand: if you corner people with guns, they will try to shoot their way out. And if you're shot at, you need to defend yourself.

'I've been shot twice. The latest time, I came out of a store on Redhills Road, I heard some shots and saw two men running towards me with guns in their hands and they also had a bag. I shouted to them, identified myself as a police officer to them, and asked them to surrender their weapons.'

The men, almost certainly recognising the huge man confronting them and realising the mess they were in, made the worst decision of their lives. They took a shot at Bigga Ford.

Bigga Ford took a shot back.

'They fired at me and I took them on and unfortunately both of them were shot and killed. The guns were recovered and also the cash that they robbed was recovered.' He shrugged. 'So, you know, you can get lucky sometimes.

'I had just gone to do some shopping and I ended up with an injury. But that's how it goes with being a police officer. Even if you are officially off duty and someone recognises you and calls on you to assist, you're automatically on duty. It's a hazard of the job. We all sign on to it and we're aware that it could happen. But we hope the good Lord can protect us most of the time.

'My family has grown with it. All they do is just pray, and hope that I'm safe. They do appreciate what I have to do. My wife is a Christian and she does believe, I think, that it's her grace and her prayers and her belief that is probably keeping me alive.'

❋   ❋   ❋

Bigga's squad work out of the Criminal Investigation Branch headquarters in downtown Kingston – a building that sounds far more impressive than it looks. Inside it's even more haphazard. None of your slick PR-friendly facade here: it has an air of neglect about it, everything a little bit on the slide, everything a touch shabby.

Entry to the Flying Squad offices themselves is through a pair of saloon doors kept wedged open – and all they have by way of a sign is a couple of yellowing A4 printed sheets.

New Scotland Yard it ain't. But beauty's skin deep – and you can't argue with a 95 per cent clear-up rate.

Bigga's office continues the theme. Long and narrow, with a desk squeezed into one end overflowing with files, bits of paper, newspaper cuttings, framed photos of his wife, good-luck trinkets, pencils, pens, notebooks, half-drunk bottles of water … If it looks chaotic, there's obviously enough method in the madness for no one to dare attempt to tidy it. On the walls are 'wanted' posters, rows of surly faces staring out in defiance or despair. Some of them have scribbled notes attached – 'Arrested', 'Shot and killed two', 'In custody', 'At large'. Others simply have big Xs through their faces: they're the ones Bigga's team didn't get to in time.

Amongst the mugshots another photo stands out – Bigga and Nelson Mandela, smiling, arms around each other. It seems the superintendent ran security for the South African president when he visited Jamaica in 1991, just a year after his release from prison. 'That was a great day,' he said, his face suddenly beaming. 'It was a great joy to shake his hand. A great day for all Kingston.'

As we took in the sights, Bigga himself manoeuvred around the mess, sinking into an enormous chair and letting out the sigh of a man who hasn't sat down for weeks.

Immediately the phones started ringing. We'd been at it for over six hours and there was no respite. Not while the gunmen were still at large. As well as the endless barrage of calls, we were constantly interrupted by boys from the squad, slipping in with scraps of paper for their boss. Everything was digested – occasionally a call was made in return. There was no panic, no rush, no screaming or hysterics. The overall impression was of a tight, slick operation revolving smoothly like a wheel – the centre of which, the pivot, the still point around which it all rotated, was Bigga Ford.

Like his headquarters, like his office, like the man himself, it's an unconventional operation. But there's no denying it works.

'Policing in Kingston is a unique skill,' he said. 'This unit I lead, our officers are in demand all over the Caribbean and the United States. I've lost six or seven persons to the United Nations. The exposure from the unit and the leadership and training does enhance your capabilities to work outside Jamaica. The skill level, their local knowledge, their training and their ability to be a team player and a team leader are all enhanced working here. The Flying Squad is an elite unit. We can ply our skills anywhere in the world.

'I've commanded other divisions, but the Flying Squad work is the most exciting aspect of all the detective stuff I've done. And I have total autonomy to go anywhere I want.'

It's that autonomy – and the vision of the new police commissioner who gave him the freedom to lead his team the way he wanted – that is giving Bigga the edge. For years the gang leaders had it easy persuading people not to trust the police – but, as we had seen for ourselves that morning, the tide was beginning to turn.

Perhaps the strangest thing of all about this enormous, unconventional cop is that his methods are straight out of the *Dixon of Dock Green* school of policing. Sure, he can handle a gun, sure he's not afraid to take a man out if he has to … but the everyday principles he's bringing to Jamaica's most elite law enforcement squad are about as basic as they come. Getting the ear of the community, gaining trust from the ordinary men and women on the street. And it's that back-to-basics approach that's sparking the kind of reaction we saw when he pulled up at the murder scene that morning. The crowds cheered him because, even in the worst ghettoes of this broken city, they know he's on their side.

'The biggest challenge is to develop sources that can give you information,' he explained, like it's the simplest thing in the world. 'Too much stuff is happening that the police don't know about. We need to go back to basics. Community policing, staying in touch with the people. The people on the street develop confidence in you as a person and then we can solve the crime.

'Is Kingston a dangerous place? I'd say no, I've been a police officer for 32 years. Yes, I've been shot, but it's all in a day's work. There are bad areas where there are people with guns, but we still have to police them. I was born and raised in the city, so I will do everything I can to make this city safe. This is my city. And if all the people who are Kingstonian feel the same way I do the city would be crime free. If there were less guns on the streets of Kingston it would be one of the best cities in the world, to live, to visit, to experience. All we're trying to do is make society more safe.'

He may be regarded as a legend on this island – and one look at the faces of the younger cops around the station make it clear that they're all in awe of him – but nobody can go on for ever. One day, maybe one day soon, Bigga Ford is going to have to retire.

He laughed at the suggestion. 'Sure, I'd like to retire. We'd all like to retire, sit in the sun, relax, watch the cricket. If you support an organisation for 32 years there must be some time in your career that you consider bowing out. So ... give me maybe another five or six years, eh? But it's been good. If I had to live my life over again, I'd probably still do it the same.

'Anyway, even then I'll be around. You don't just walk away. I'll still pass on the information I get. I'll still have the contacts within the organisation.

'Will there be a replacement for me? Yes, man, there'll be a replacement. I'm working on it right now. I'm an old-school Kingston cop. I've been identifying suitable young police officers to mentor, so we'll take them, introduce them to the people, and they'll develop their relations and contacts, so in future they can serve the organisation, the community, like I have. That's the way it works, man.'

We were interrupted by two vital bits of news. First, the cricket scores ('What? You joke? They cannot bat! What's wrong wit them?') and then more serious business. The names of our shooters have been checked out – and the feeling was they're good, likely candidates. The Flying Squad was getting ready to fly again.

✳   ✳   ✳

In a room at the end of the corridor outside Bigga's office, 12 men and women sat around shooting the breeze, swapping anecdotes and stories. Most of them were wearing flak jackets – those who weren't would be soon. One man idly twirled an M16 gun barrel on the floor as he listened to another describe the football match he'd seen the night before.

The room itself was stuffy, windowless. A bank of fans were working flat out, but only moving the stale air around. It all made for a strange combination of the relaxed and the tense – a combination we'd seen in squad rooms before, always before a big takedown.

Suddenly the conversations ceased, and as the massive bulk of Bigga Ford slowly made its way into the centre of the gathering, everyone stood.

'I'll keep it brief,' he said. 'We know what's occurred, where we're going. Instruction has come that we need to give some extra special presence in the area. We're getting some information as to who the shooters are. I'm asking everyone to wear their vests and be careful. I cannot afford to lose another officer, especially from this unit.'

There's silent, tacit agreement, and the last of the officers picked up their body armour.

'So as soon as I finish speaking you need to get your arms and your vests and hit the road,' continued Bigga. 'We're still after two out of the three gunmen.'

Then, as rifles were shouldered, magazines checked, bullets counted, he turned to us. 'We got work to do now,' he said. 'I got my team to look after.'

And right then, his team was the superintendent's number one priority. We had joined him as he clocked on that morning, accompanied him on a frantic race through rush-hour traffic barely an hour later. We'd seen the dead boy sprawled in the dust, heard about the policeman in the morgue – and we'd watched as the crowd in the ghetto chanted Bigga's name like he was a conquering hero. We'd stuck with him as he cruised the avenues and alleyways for information, saw the respect he commands and gives out on the street. We'd spent the rest of the day with him in his cramped office, as he put the pieces together, solving the crime. And now, as the sun dipped down behind Spanish Town and the inland mountains, we had minutes left with this one-off, larger-than-life cop before setting off to catch a flight out of Jamaica. It had been an eye-opener, to say the least.

'Not all the days start like this,' he smiled. 'Though of course some of the days do. My job is a lot of hard work and dedication – but today is not an average day. We'll probably keep going on this one straight through into the night. It's hard work but we're up to it. We want Jamaica to be a safe place.

'This job: it's not a nine-to-five, you know? There's no sleep, no rest. Even at home the phone will just be going on, going on …'

As if on cue, his two mobiles started up, and we said our goodbyes and split. We had a plane to catch: and Cornwall Bigga Ford, superintendent of the Jamaica Flying Squad, had a cop killer to take down. His team beat us out of the door, screaming off in their cars, armed and armoured, and we left Bigga alone in his squad room, eyeing up an M16 rifle, waiting for one call in particular.

'As soon as we get that call we go in as a team,' he said. 'And when we do get the call I'll go too. My boys have got to know that the boss is in there with them.'

BOYZ IN THE HOOD:
ON THE 77TH WITH RON LOPEZ

The City of Angels. The last stop. This place is also my adopted home; these streets are my streets.

Except they're not. Not really. This may be where I live – but where we were going was a different world. On any ordinary day you won't catch me strolling the sidewalks of South Central LA.

Made famous by rappers and riots, South Central includes some of the worst neighbourhoods in America. The streets here are crawling with gangs – shootings, assaults, drugs and robbery are all just a part of daily life.

In the heart of it all, surrounded on all sides, is the 77th Precinct Gang Unit, led by Sergeant Ron Lopez. This is their problem … so naturally we expected them to be a proper crew of hard bastards, used to wading in first and asking questions later. We were going to be surprised. Ron was going to give us a lesson on understanding gang culture – and how to use it to get real, solid results.

Knowledge is power, they say. And I don't think I've ever met anyone as straight-up sussed as Ron Lopez.

✸   ✸   ✸

IT WAS CLOSE TO MIDNIGHT in South Central LA, and Sergeant Ron Lopez had just handed me a nightstick.

A black-and-white patrol car had seen a party going on where it wasn't supposed to be – attended by people who shouldn't have been there. It was the cue for Lopez and his team from the 77th Precinct Gang Unit to roll. As he hooked up with another couple of cars and we all took off together, hurtling through the streets, Lopez needed both hands on the wheel. And that meant giving us his truncheon to look after.

We were glad of any kind of weapon. If Los Angeles is notorious as the home of modern American gang culture, then South Central LA is where the worst of it goes down. We'd seen enough hip-hop videos, picked up the lyrics to enough gangsta rap songs and watched enough movies to know that this was the real deal. These streets don't suffer fools at the best of times – and crashing a gang party in the heart of the 'hood is never something you're going to want to do with just your wits for defence.

The nightstick was a beast. Two feet long, at least an inch wide, solid black fibreglass. A smack from this and you'd know about it.

'Every actor should have one of these,' I said, with a grin, hefting its weight and slapping it against my palm.

Ron swung the car round another bend at breakneck speed. 'You would get more parts,' he deadpanned. 'Take that to your auditions.'

As we moved through the streets, he explained exactly what was about to go down. The black-and-white had called in a gathering of about 30 known gang members outside a house in the 77th district – there was music, drinking, possible drug-taking … but most of all, the partygoers included boys who were on probation or parole. They were not supposed to be hanging out together: and that made it an illegal get-together. Ron's gang unit were going to break it up.

'It's causing a disturbance for the neighbours,' he said. 'They got loud music, stuff like that. But the other reason for breaking up gang parties is it gives rival gangs a good target. So we can disperse the party before they actually become victims of crime from the rival gangs.

'If everybody is still there, then it should be a pretty good hit. They saw a lot of gangsters congregating.'

We'd been in LA a couple of days, but this was the first really dangerous situation we'd been a part of. A party just didn't meant drinking and drugs – in this neck of the woods it meant guns.

'All of the above are very likely in a situation like this,' confirmed Ron. 'What we'll be paying specific attention to is looking for one or two guys that try to make a break for it on the back side of the group – it's not the drinking so much. But any time you get people with too much booze in them, liquid courage, they think they are tougher than they are. You throw in drugs on top of it – it has the potential to be very dangerous.'

Ron had a glint in his eye – and when we had met with the other men from his unit before heading out here they all had the same air about them – excitement. Adrenaline. They were up for it, they lived for action like this.

Ron laughed. 'This is like a kid going to Disneyland for them,' he said. 'They affectionately refer to it as "smashing". It's where you go smash a party. While it's inherently dangerous, for the adrenaline junkie it gets you amped up a little bit. It's what these guys really enjoy. Plus they are making a big difference. If they can go in and break up this party, we take a few guys to jail, we recover a few guns, those guns can't be used for shootings down the road, right? You don't have to worry about some innocent little kid walking across a street getting hit by a stray bullet. And that's the real reason why we do what we do. Hopefully it pans out.'

There were five cars in our convoy: we were in the lead vehicle. That made, what, 10 of us?

'Eight guys,' said Ron.

Eight guys against 30?

He laughed again, before killing the lights and slowing the car down to a stop. We were nearly there: the wide suburban streets of South Central LA were dark and ominous, the spaces between streetlights filled with menace. The party was just around the corner and we could hear the music already – something fast, aggressive, a man spitting out raps against a barrage of beats and breaks.

'Eight against 30 seems pretty fair to me,' whispered Ron, still smiling. 'Nine if you count me – and if we count you, Vin, it's 10.'

'Eleven,' I said and held up the nightstick. 'Me and my mate here.'

Ron didn't reply – just one glance in the rear-view to check his boys were all with him, and then a foot on the gas and a squeal of tyres and we were there.

Three dozen guys and girls were hanging out in the backyard of a house, where a couple of trestle tables had been set out with drinks and food on, and a stereo was banging out the gangsta rap we had heard. Next moment there was shouting, running, the cars unloaded and the 10 of us barged in amongst them. The music was killed, everyone ordered to get their hands up and get them up NOW. More shouting, protests, hands on holsters … and eventually, slouching, grumbling, taking their own sweet time, they did as they were told.

A little too easily, to be honest. It didn't seem right. And apart from the fact that we were deep in the 'hood and every single one of these people had a look in their eyes of pure contempt for anyone associated with the LAPD, it all just seemed a little bit … safe.

Not that this stopped Ron's men. 'Against the wall!' they shouted, and everyone was lined up and made to assume the position as they were frisked. Ron and another cop ducked inside and searched the house. We hung back with the nightstick.

Some of the boys with their hands up against the chainlink were laughing. We found nothing. Whatever was here had gone – and the gangsters Ron was after had gone with them.

✼   ✼   ✼

Los Angeles was our last stop on this trip. And it was a sort of homecoming for me: for the past few years LA has been my adopted home town. It's the second largest city in the United States, the centre of the film industry, and home to some of the most beautiful and glamorous people on the planet.

Everyone knows about Rodeo Drive, Sunset Boulevard and Venice Beach, but beyond the designer labels, hard bodies and whitened teeth there's another side to the city. LA may be the showbiz capital of the world, but scrape away the glitz and glamour and you're left with an underbelly of crime and violence.

It's a side I don't see too much of – nobody would want to, given the choice. But everyone who lives in LA knows about the South Central area, even if they make sure never to be found there. Taking in the notorious communities of Compton and Inglewood, South Central is home to the city's black and Latino gangs and for most citizens has become a no-go area, even a war zone. Gang crime is rife here, and violence, shootings and murders are just a part of everyday life.

The two most infamous gangs are the Bloods and the Crips. The Crips emerged in the early 1970s and are identifiable by their blue colours. The Bloods, whose colour is red, were formed a few years later to rival the Crips. For years they carved up these streets between them – but now they're getting outnumbered by the Hispanic gangs, who are proving themselves every bit as ruthless when it comes to defending their territory.

In 1992 the gang violence exploded into real war. Four LAPD officers had been accused of brutality against a black motorist called Rodney King; when they were acquitted – despite videos of them appearing to beat King being shown on television – Armageddon came to the South Central Los Angeles as the worst rioting America had ever witnessed was played out on these streets.

For six days, thousands of Angelinos ran wild. There was widespread looting, arson and violence. Two thousand people were injured and 53 were killed. The cost of damage to property was estimated at $1 billion. Nearly 4,000 separate fires were set and 1,100 buildings were destroyed – during the height of the lawlessness calls to the fire brigade were coming faster than one every minute.

The police couldn't cope. The National Guard had to be called in – and when they too were overwhelmed, the US Army and the Marines were sent on to the streets.

Eventually, order was restored – but the price was high. As well as the dead and injured, the area itself had been ripped apart, destroyed by the very people who had to live there. And even once regeneration began, buildings were rebuilt and investment poured into the area, the gangs remained.

So bad is South Central's image that in 2003 city officials even changed the name of the area to simply South Los Angeles: hoping the new title would help overcome the region's terrible reputation. Street signs were altered and the media instructed not to refer to South Central again … but it hasn't worked. Talk about

South LA and nobody really knows where you mean – talk about South Central and you're talking gangs.

In the past five years alone these streets have witnessed over 23,000 gang-related crimes – and in the last 25 years more than 10,000 gang members have been killed.

It's worth saying that again: 10,000. That's an army; in fact, it's more than the total number of British troops in Afghanistan at the time we were in LA. And don't forget: those 10,000 were just the casualties of this war – the ones who've ended up dead. The numbers of those shot and shooting, stabbed and stabbing, robbed and robbing, pushing, pimping … well it just gets scary.

The highest concentration of gang activity in the city is in the 77th district, an area lying roughly between LAX airport and downtown LA, deep in Inglewood. These are not streets I would ever normally tread. And so, for my final outing with the world's toughest cops, that's exactly where I was headed.

✻   ✻   ✻

Before I did anything, however, I wanted to get an idea of exactly what I would be facing. I hooked up with two of LAPD's finest – men who have seen it all and done it all, cops who have dedicated the best part of their lives to confronting the gangs head on.

First up was Commander Pat Gannon, head of all the gang units in the LAPD. We met him outside the shiny, imposing police building downtown – and he didn't waste any time or words in explaining the scale of the problem.

'There are hundreds of gangs in the city of Los Angeles,' he told us. 'And they're in the south part of the city. For example, in South Los Angeles, in one small 10-square-mile area there are 60 gangs – with 60 subsets of those particular gangs.'

Sixty gangs within 60 gangs? We didn't even bother working out what 60 times 60 was. And this was just in a 10-mile block?

'In a 10-mile area,' he confirmed. 'The problem has evolved over a period of time. But for Los Angeles it's really when cocaine, crack cocaine, PCP and those types of drugs became very prevalent. And then you had the selling of those drugs ... and that became a moneymaker.'

There were gangs before there was crack and PCP to sell – but it was the drugs that changed the game. If the gangs started as a means of forging a collective identity, with people of the same background getting together and sticking together for security and even community, then once the idea of criminal competition took hold, there was no going back. Put at its simplest: the gangs led to crime, the crime led to violence, the violence has led to murder ... and it just keeps getting worse. Becoming part of a gang means swearing undying loyalty to that brotherhood – and declaring war on any rival gangs. Or sometimes even subsets within your gang.

Why? Commander Pat Gannon thinks he knows the answer.

'I'll tell you what they always talk about,' he said with something like a sarcastic smile. 'They always say it's about the neighbourhoods, about protecting their own.' He shook his head. 'No. It's not all for the neighbourhood. It's about money.'

The commander introduced us to Dan Horan, an LAPD officer with 27 years of experience policing the gangs of South Central. He works the 77th district – named after the location of the station or precinct – an area which takes in some of the worst trouble the area has to offer.

We had been set up to meet Sergeant Ron Lopez, who heads up the 77th Gang Unit: we would be out on this beat before too long. We asked Dan if he had one piece of advice.

'You have got to be ready,' he said. 'Even though it's calm right now, within blocks of us there are a lot of people who are criminals. Gangsters who like to shoot each other, people who commit robberies and other violent crime. Anything can change at a moment's notice. The radio can all of a sudden say there is a robbery in progress, there is a shooting in progress. You know: you're sitting in an intersection and next thing you know you're in a car chase.

'They might be carrying guns, so when you walk up on any car you really have to be on your toes. They could have a gun and you wouldn't know it until you are right up next to them. So for 27 years I have never got rid of the butterflies. Especially walking up on a car – and especially when it's driven by a couple of gangsters.'

This year alone the LAPD have confiscated 3,600 illegal weapons – but Dan reckons that, in the 77th at least, they really are making a difference.

'As of today,' he said, with something like pride in his voice, 'in the 77th division – that's 11 square miles – we have had 17 murders this year. And probably 10 or 15 years ago for the year we had over 160. If we could finish the year with less then 35 that borders on the miraculous.'

Before we left for our meeting with Ron Lopez and a chance to get out on the streets for real, Dan thought of another piece of advice.

'When you do make a mistake you better learn from it,' he said. 'Hopefully you survive it. In your field, in the movies, if you make a mistake … you know, there's always Take Two. Around here you make a mistake and there is no more Take Two. You know what I'm saying?'

We did. Loud and clear. We left Pat and Dan and prepared to hook up with Ron Lopez, both scared and excited at the same time. Scared ... because this was my home town. Any bad boys we met could theoretically at least track me down, find out where I live, get in a cab and be outside my front door in less than an hour – and that would not be good. And excited ... because this was my home town. This was the problem on my doorstep. This was what I saw on the local news every night. And besides: by the sound of it, the boys from the 77th weren't the kind to hold back when the shit was going down. And that's always got to be a buzz.

✿　　✿　　✿

We met Ron in his office at the 77th precinct. He was tall – my height at least, and about my weight too – with slicked black hair and dark, steady eyes. Still only in his mid-thirties, he's clocked up 14 years on the force – and his youthful looks hide a wealth of experience on the front line.

The thing about Ron is – he's smart. He's got a lot of knowledge. He could do a PhD in the gangs of South Central ... he could do it in his sleep. The walls of his office are covered in street maps and mugshots, a rogues' gallery of known gang members, wanted suspects, recent convictions, parolees, probationers and all-round bad guys.

We watched in increasing confusion as he ran a hand over them. He thought he was explaining the situation to us – but after about the first sentence we were lost.

'OK,' he said, with a grin. 'I'll go slow. These guys,' and he indicated a set of faces pinned against the map, 'These guys are Bloods. Part of the Bloods gang.' We were with him so far – but then as he warmed up, his hand was all over the map, pointing out different mugshots, different streets ... 'These here are Bloods too. Bloods ... these are Bloods, these Bloods too. These ones –

they're Crips. And then within the Crips there is two different sets of Crips. Neighbourhood Crips and gangster Crips. They're very different: even though they are both called Crips they don't get along, they will fight each other just like a Crip would fight like a Blood. So ... these guys are neighbourhood, these are neighbourhood ... neighbourhood ... these are neighbourhood Crips as well.

'Now. These gangs all have trouble with the Hoovers.' He waved an arm at another part of the map. All these streets, these gang divisions, so fiercely contested and defended, were right next to each other. 'Hoovers are gangster Crips. These are Hoover streets, so are these, and these. So these guys will fight these guys. Just as much as they would fight these guys. You follow?'

No.

We tried a different tactic. The maps were covered in stickers: each street labelled with the name of the gang who controlled it. We asked him if there was any history behind the gang names.

'Most of them are geographic, after what street they live off of,' he said. 'So, like "Six Deuce" means 62nd Street. "Seven Tray" means 73rd Street. They aren't very creative when it comes to that. "Eighteenth Street", which is one of our Hispanic gangs, started on 18th Street.'

So which was the oldest gang?

'The oldest here in the 77th is probably going to be the 60's,' he said. 'The Rolling 60's. They are definitely the biggest, with 1500 documented members. There is a rite of passage to become a member. Either they get jumped in or they have to do some sort of crime to show their worth – a robbery or a shooting or something to that effect. They're active from the get-go. Earn their stripes so to speak.'

We wanted to know what getting jumped in meant.

'It's an initiation,' he explained. 'Where three, four, five guys will tune them up for three or four minutes. They don't usually put them in hospital, though. It just depends how bad the beating is. Usually they try not to because it negates the point.'

We looked again at the wallpaper of surly faces and outlined streets. It still wasn't making too much sense. It was about to get more complicated.

'So, these all get updated, all right?' explained Ron, before helpfully pointing out a couple of faces in particular. 'So these guys are in custody. And this guy just got killed in a shooting five days ago.

'Over the last few days it's been busy, with shootings back and forth. The shootings have been between the Eight Tray gangsters and Rolling 60's. They have been enemies for 30-plus years. The 60's send people in to shoot them … 60's or 90's will send guys in there.' He was back on to the map again, finger flicking from one street to the next. 'You see the 40's, 60's and 90's all get along. They're all neighbourhoods, just like the 55's, 57's, 58's – they all get along. They're all neighbourhood sets. So they're all buddies.'

In which case, the answer was simple, wasn't it? If you're all just doing your own thing in your own street, why not leave it at that? Why deliberately go into another gang's turf and start shooting at them?

Ron laughed, as if we had finally grasped the point. 'If we could figure that out …' he said, before adding, 'Call it reputation. They do it for reputation. And you know what? Cos it's easy.'

The fact was: we didn't have a hope of understanding the situation on paper. All these gang names, all these streets, these faces on the wall – it was too much to take in. We had to see it in action, at ground level. It was time to stop talking and start walking.

Or rather, driving.

* * *

As we pulled out of the precinct car park and headed on to the streets, Ron kept talking. There were five cars from his gang unit today, all cruising around, eyes and ears open, ready to react. Nobody knew what the day would bring – like Dan Horan had told us, the point about this neighbourhood was that things could change at any moment. So many gangs in such a small area meant trouble was never too long in coming.

Ron drove slowly, concentrating on every face we passed. The streets were busy enough, kids were hanging out or else slouching slowly along in that weird, stiff-legged, shuffling walk the boys here have … at first we thought it was something to do with their baggy jeans, the way they wore them down halfway round their arses – we later found out the real reason. The Crips name itself comes from 'cripples' – and the walk has its roots in the original Crips' mimicking of the way someone crippled might move. See a homeboy shuffling down the street like that – round here the chances are he's a Crip.

We found something else out too: the loose pants weren't just a fashion thing. They were originally a sign that you'd done time in prison. When the cops arrest you, they remove anything from your clothes that could be used as a weapon or a means of suicide – and that includes your belt.

As we checked out the neighbourhood, Ron filled us in on his own background.

He always wanted to be a cop; there was never any question of doing anything else. Ron's father served for 38 years with the LAPD, so it wasn't like he came into the force without knowing the risks. He reckons it's in his blood.

'For us the earliest you can come on the job is 20 and a half – because you have to be 21 when you graduate from the Academy and it's a seven-month course,' he explained. 'So the day after I turned 20 and a half I went and took the test. I've been doing the job for a little over 14 years now – and I've been in the gang unit a little over two years.

'This was actually all I thought I was ever gonna do. In high school when you meet with the guidance counsellor, and he asks, you know, what do you want to be when you grow up? I told him I was gonna be a cop.'

What about his wife and kids? Ron's dad might have notched up nearly four decades on the beat, but there's no denying that these streets are a whole lot more dangerous than they were 20 years ago. It was a different ball game now: more drugs, more gangs, more guns. And respect for police officers is not exactly forthcoming in these parts.

'I sacrifice a lot of time away from the family, but in the long run it is better for them,' he said. 'I have the same routine every day before I go to work. I kiss the kids goodbye every single day – whether they're happy with their dad at the time or not. And my wife has been with me since just before I started working, so this is all she has ever known me doing. And she has family that was on the job too: her uncle is retired LAPD. So she has a little bit of understanding of some of the things we deal with.

'But yeah, she still gives me a call before she goes to bed. She likes me to shoot her a text message when I'm on the way home, so she knows where I'm at.'

Everyone's wife worries a little about their other half's job though, right? I've known footballers whose wives couldn't watch them play in case they got injured – and even now, when I'm on a set and there's stunts to be done, my wife is always telling me to be careful. But this was different. There are people in these streets who would happily shoot Ron and his colleagues dead. There are people out here who think about doing that every single day.

'Well ...' He thought about that for a moment. 'She was opposed to me working gangs. I had the opportunity back in 1998 to go work the gang unit as an officer, not as a supervisor, and because of her concern, and the fact that we had just had our first child, I turned down the spot and stayed in just regular patrol. But when I was offered this position, I basically turned around and I told her: "I've turned it down once, I'm not turning it down again." Opportunities like this don't come around very often. The 77th is arguably the most elite gang unit in the entire city of LA. Out of 21 divisions – not to toot our own horn – but we're probably the cream of the crop.

'Our unit has taken more guns off the street than any other gang unit in the entire city. Last year we took almost 200 guns off the street, the year before we took 250. I think this year we're at about 120 so far, which means in two and a half years that's almost 500 guns we've taken off the street. We're batting at an average of one every two days.'

He grinned again. 'But there is always the potential. There is always the potential for that spark that's going to get the embers going and have something flare up. It could happen any time.'

It was about to happen now.

✵   ✵   ✵

Two incidents happened in quick succession, one after the other. The first was pretty relaxed – the second anything but.

We were still in the area known as the 60s – after the grid of numbered streets that made up the neighbourhood – when the radio crackled and Ron picked up the call. Another of his units had spotted a known gang member acting suspiciously as they drove past his house – he had stepped out of the door, scoped the cops and immediately ducked back inside, slamming the door behind him.

The cops were out of the car and into the house straight after him. When we arrived they had him in custody and were turning the place over. Ron introduced us to Steve McClean, a shortish, solid guy with a shaved head. He showed us around.

'This is one of our regular stops we check on here,' he said. The place didn't look too bad – not as bad as some of the buildings we'd seen. Just a run-of-the-mill apartment block – I've been in more intimidating looking places in East London. The looks, however, weren't the point. 'This is notorious for selling drugs back here,' continued Steve. 'We've been in this particular apartment before for weapons violations.' He pointed towards one of the windows. 'We've recovered assault rifles from this room. Anyway we came down here today, we recognised the probationer stepping out of the house and slamming the door back. There was a strong smell of marijuana.'

Steve and his partner had chased the man inside but they hadn't been quick enough. 'He flushed it,' he said. 'We heard the toilet flush. And that's where we are right now, we got nothing. We have cleared the house of people, searched it and … nothing.'

We didn't want to sound funny or anything, but … what if there was nothing to find?

Steve just laughed at us. 'This is the 60s neighbourhood, Blood gang area,' said Ron, shaking his head. 'And he is a documented gang member. We know him, he sells dope for the gang.'

'Today he stays out,' shrugged Steve. 'We'll catch him next week.'

It seemed a bit crazy that they knew exactly what this guy was up to, that he was a known Blood, that he was selling drugs for the Bloods … and yet Ron and Steve still couldn't find anything to pin on him. But this cat-and-mouse game is all part of the job. The cops try to stay one step ahead of the bad guys … and the bad guys try to stay one step ahead of the cops.

'Oh, it's amazing how much intelligence criminals have,' said Ron – meaning the information kind of intelligence, as well as the brains kind. 'They've become very savvy over the years. Some criminals have family members in law enforcement who for some reason or another will provide them insight. Sometimes they'll just call the front desk at the station and they'll say they know me; they'll say, "Hey, is Sergeant Lopez working today?" – and if the desk guy's not paying attention he'll tell them.'

Today's man had – nearly – been caught out by the gang units' own form of counter-intelligence.

'Sometimes we'll switch our start times, just to try and keep them on their toes, so to speak,' explained Ron. 'Like today for example: normally today we would start at 2 p.m. – so today we started at midday. When you look at it from a numbers point of view we're always outnumbered, always outgunned. So we got to think creatively.'

Phoning the station, though – I couldn't help it: I had to smile. You had to admire the front of it. Cheeky buggers.

And talking of cheeky buggers …

We thought there was something a little odd about Steve's accent: it turned out we had something in common. He was another ex-pat Brit who'd set up home in LA. After a stint in the British army he came over here and joined up with the local cops. We asked him where in England he was from originally.

'Brighton,' he told us – and when I mentioned that I used to run my greyhounds at Brighton dogs, he gave us a wink. 'Is that right? I imagine my brother wasted some money on your dogs, then. He's into his dogs, horses, football …'

Playing or betting?

'Both,' he said, before patting me on the back and laughing. 'He's a dirty player on the pitch – just like you.'

Like I said: cheeky bugger.

* * *

We were only just back in the vehicle and still laughing about Steve when another call came through. Ron listened for a moment, before punching the car into drive. A couple of kids had been spotted selling drugs, and their reaction on seeing the cops had been the same as the guy Steve had just chased … but without a nearby toilet to flush the stash down, one of them had done something very stupid.

We powered through the streets and pulled up behind a paramedic truck. Ron jumped out and immediately assessed the situation. Right now the bust itself wasn't the real issue – it was the health of the kid who had tried to get rid of the drugs.

The cops had jumped out on him and, desperate to get rid of the evidence, he'd stuck the lot in his mouth and swallowed. Before anyone could get their fingers in his throat, it was all gone … and right now, the effect would be kicking in.

He was a skinny thing, all arms and legs: if he was even a teenager yet he didn't look it. With wide, yellowing eyes, he sat on the stretcher and didn't say a word … whether it was from fear, the effects of the bag of crack cocaine he'd just necked, or a simple, reflex hatred of cops, we couldn't tell. Despite the heat of afternoon LA, he started to shiver.

Just then there was a commotion on the sidewalk behind us. A man had turned up and started shouting at the boy. 'Hey! You swallowed some dope?' he yelled.

Ron went over to calm him down – it turned out this was the boy's dad. He didn't look like a gangster – and he didn't look best pleased to see his son surrounded by cops and paramedics. 'Did you swallow some dope?' he shouted again.

The kid couldn't even meet his eyes.

'I'll take that look away as guilt then,' said Ron.

The man ignored him. As the boy was bundled into the ambulance and taken to have his stomach pumped, and we prepared to move on, he just stayed put, shouting at whoever would listen. 'My son ain't swallowed no dope! I don't care what you say. But I know my son ain't swallowed no fucking drugs!'

Drug crime is an ongoing battle for the cops in LA. Latest figures show that seizures of cocaine are up 150 per cent, marijuana 200 per cent and methamphetamine a staggering 1000 per cent. And you would think this is a good sign, right? It means the cops are getting more of it off the street.

Well, sort of. Seizures are up because the cops are confiscating more – that's true. But they're also up because there's more out there. And when you've got kids as young as the one we had just seen peddling crack on street corners, how do you even start to combat that?

We asked Ron if he thought pop culture was partly to blame. The movies and music videos that glamorised the gang scene – did they influence the younger kids to get involved with the gangs?

Ron reckoned it was a bit trickier than that. 'To an extent it glamorises it,' he said, 'but then a lot of what they portray is true. Some rappers are actual legitimate gang members that have kind of crossed over – and then there are other rappers that pretend to be gangsters but they never really were true gang members. If you see in a rap video, guys hanging out, drinking beers in a backyard, that's normal, and it's something you'd see down here. If you see them cruising through the streets, that's something you'd see them do. If you see them waving guns around, all that type of stuff ... that's a little bit of fluff. Call it dramatising it for the camera.

'The gangsters will hype it up for certain TV programmes. Like if you guys came in here on your own and said you're doing a documentary, they'll bring their guns out and show them to you, that type of stuff. But just for them to be standing out on the street waving their guns, it doesn't happen like that, not like a video would portray.'

But 13-year-old kids selling crack ... that wasn't hype. That was nothing short of tragic. But the really sad thing is that, in these parts, it's also so ordinary it barely registers any more.

✿   ✿   ✿

We were back in the car, back on the streets, back rolling around the 'hood looking for trouble.

What was strange, however, was that despite the reputation this place has, despite all we'd seen on the news and all the statistics we'd been shown ... South Central LA didn't actually look that bad. In Baltimore, for example, we knew exactly when we were getting into the bad districts – the boarded-up houses, the empty lots, the smashed windows and faceless buildings, the sheer number of homeless people littering the streets like shambling bags of rags – but this place just wasn't like that.

The roads here are wide, lined with trees. Houses are mostly detached, set back from the sidewalk, with gardens out front. And sure, there were occasional knots of people, groups of kids hanging out on corners ... but nothing like the swarms of troublemakers we saw in other gang-infested areas.

To be honest, at first glance it all seemed pretty safe and quiet. Suburban. These weren't slums, this wasn't anything like the shanty towns, barrios and urban wastelands we'd seen in other cities around the world.

But like they say: location, location, location. Make no mistake – in terms of crime levels, this is as bad a place as you'll find anywhere in the United States.

As we cruised through the 60s, Ron quickly set us straight on that score. In fact, in his calm, easygoing way, he was about to give us a social history lesson on LA gang culture.

'The thing is, down here it's inundated with gangs no matter where you turn,' he said. 'On any street or in any house.' He pointed at a pair of wide bungalows. 'Like, look at these two houses right here, really nice houses – new, freshly built: if they were in your neck of the woods they'd cost about a million dollars, in my neck of the woods probably about $600,000 … here, more like $350,000.

'But would you buy it? You might have a very nice-looking house, you might see families with little kids and puppies and stuff in the front yard … but there's still the gang element within the neighbourhood. Everywhere. You used to hear horror stories about people who would put their kids to sleep in their bathtub – so when the bullets started flying every night they wouldn't have to worry about their kids getting shot.'

Property might be cheap round here, but what's the point of owning a swanky house if you're too scared to step out of the front door? Or if there's a chance of a bullet coming through your window?

'A lot of the people in this neighbourhood still live in a tremendous amount of fear of the gangs,' he said. 'Especially if they've been down here for 10, 15, 20 years, because they remember what it was like. They know how violent it can get.

'Also, a lot of this area changed after the riots in 1992 – because the vast majority of this area was destroyed, the businesses were all vandalised, grocery stores were all set on fire, things like that. There was a big resurgence in the neighbourhood after that, though it took a few years for it to happen. From 1992 to 1998 this was kind of like a ghost town, and then you had people dumping money in, new businesses coming in … and that's why there's so many nice-looking new properties.'

The houses might be new – but a lot of the problems remain. As we continued to drive, Ron kept up his commentary – and was now illustrating his points with examples.

'So this area that we're in right now is Six Deuce Brims territory – Six Deuce for 62nd Street, right? They're one of the most active Bloods gangs.' He pointed towards a building on the left. 'This apartment complex here is like their stronghold.'

It didn't look like a gang stronghold. It was in good nick, there were palm trees lining the sidewalk outside … it was the sort of place that in a different area would be considered pretty des res. The only difference was the kids hanging round outside. Five or six of them, none older than 14, dressed in baggy T-shirts, long shorts and trainers – and every one of them staring right at us. Those weren't friendly looks. They may only have been kids, but between you and me, I was a little bit intimidated by them myself.

'All of these people here are either gangsters or gangsters' family,' confirmed Ron, slowing to a crawl as we passed them – making sure they could see him checking them out. 'Every single one of them. And that young kid standing on the corner – we just arrested his brother four days ago for robbery.'

No wonder he was shooting us such a dirty look. We asked who he had robbed. Like a mugging, or a housebreaking?

Ron laughed. 'He actually robbed his mother, believe it or not. He got into a fight with his mom, punched her, threw her down on the ground and ripped her necklace off and took her rent money out of her pocket.

'He had a gun on him during the robbery, and his little brother there – we found this out after the fact – he passed the gun to his little brother and he ran and hid it before we got here. Actually as we were running up the stairs to go to the apartment, his little brother ran down the other hallway and hid the gun.'

Ron gave him a wave. The kid stood with his hands in his pockets and scowled.

Guns. It was always about guns. And round here getting a gun is as easy as making a phone call.

'The vast majority of the guns that are out on the street are stolen,' said Ron. 'Almost every gang has got that one guy: you call him up and say, "Hey, Vinnie, I need a gun," and he'll be able to get you one – or he'll be "go to the first house on the corner, look under the front porch and find what you need" – that type of thing.'

Although these boys tend to favour handguns – easier to hide down a pair of shorts, easier to get rid of – Ron remembered one incident where the weapon in question was in a different class altogether.

'We were monitoring a gang funeral – we had two of my guys dressed in plain clothes and in an unmarked van, just watching over with binoculars and seeing who was coming and going. And they see a pick-up truck right out in front of the funeral parlour that they kept on going to. We finally decided to move in, and inside the truck were two handguns and an AR15, which is the civilian model of the M16 that the military carries. It had a 100-round drum magazine and a silencer on it.

'If those gangsters had decided to shoot it out we could have had five or six cops shot or killed with that gun – it had the ability to go fully automatic like a military gun. They would have been able to put 30, 40 rounds down on us before we could even figure out what had happened, cos of the silencer.'

He had another story, too. This was even more frightening.

'We had an eight-year-old girl got killed about a year ago,' said Ron. 'And that one was sheer stupidity. Her family is from one particular gang and her cousin is from another gang. Her own cousin came over to do the shooting and instead of hitting the adult cousin, he hit his eight-year-old cousin and killed her.'

Why would anyone want to shoot their own cousin? Because gang ties are stronger than family ties – and because, round here, getting a reputation as a shooter gives you instant cred where it matters.

'Anybody who would go out and actually shoot someone has instant credibility amongst their gang,' he confirmed. 'Not every gang member has the guts or the backbone to go out and do a shooting. To actually get out of a car and walk up and actually shoot someone. Not many people have that ability.

'The sad thing is, it's increasingly the younger guys. If they're juvenile and get caught it's not as bad as if they're an adult. If you're a 15-year-old kid and you go do a shooting, and the guy doesn't die, you'll maybe do a year or two in juvenile camp. If you're 18, 19 years old, and you do the same exact shooting, you'll go down for three or four years in jail. So for the older guys, it's easier to recruit the younger, up-and-coming gangsters. They'll say OK, you want to earn your stripes: go out and do it.'

We took a last look at the kids outside the Six Deuce Brims base – and we couldn't help wondering how many of them would have that backbone.

* * *

Back to the action. Steve radioed in – there was something he wanted us to see. He had pulled over another couple of gang members on a routine stop-and-search, and one of them had an especially fine example of the tattoos they use to identify themselves. Ron drove us over there.

Now I've got some tatts myself – but nothing like these. This boy had taken his declaration of loyalty way above and beyond the call of duty.

He was leaning against a wall when we arrived, and Steve stood in front of him, with that same mischievous grin on his face. As we approached he gave him a tap on the shoulder. 'Here we go,' he said, 'show us what you got.'

The gang member was another youngster, still in his teens, dressed in the usual T-shirt and baggy jeans combo. He was bare-foot – Steve had made him take his trainers off when he searched him – and, although he was doing his best to look defiant for us, he also seemed pretty out of it. Whether it was drink or drugs we couldn't say … but either way he'd had something that was giving him a bit of Dutch courage.

He watched us through half-closed eyes. And then as we looked for whatever Steve wanted to show us, he suddenly shut his eyes completely.

What the …? There was something horribly wrong there, something had messed up his eyelids. We peered closer – and realised he'd had them tattooed. On each lid, in a kind of gothic-style font, there was a big black number.

I couldn't even imagine how much that must have hurt. Getting your arm done can smart a bit – and that's where the skin is thick. But your eyelids? Just the thought of someone with a tattoo needle anywhere near my eyes made me a bit wobbly. No wonder the kid was half-cut.

'This is Darren,' said Steve. Darren opened his eyes and shut them again. 'Darren just got these put on. That's brand new. When did you get them put on, bruv?'

Darren kept his eyes shut. It was too weird looking at him, with those black numbers glaring back at us.

'I can't tell you that,' he muttered. 'They say Six-Seven.'

Six-Seven? What does that mean?

He snapped his eyes open again and sneered: 'Neighbourhood Crips.'

Steve pointed out a couple more of Darren's gang markings – thankfully these were located a bit more traditionally on his arm and shoulder. They were all pretty much variations on the Six-Seven theme … except for a couple we couldn't read that had big Xs tattooed through them.

'He got these put on when he was about what … 14? He went to a boot camp when my partner was an instructor there. Anyway, part of the deal was he got his tattoos removed. And here he is: still hanging out.' He shrugged, as if to say, yeah, nice one, that obviously worked, before pointing at the big Xs. 'Here he has his rival gangs' hand signs wacked out. They're Hoovers. That basically means fuck the Hoovers.'

Darren kept opening and shutting his eyes, flicking between those numbers and his dark, glazed pupils. I asked him what it was like being on the street.

He coughed, shifted his feet. 'It's not bad,' he said.

What about the guns? Are there a lot of shootings on the streets?

Suddenly he was more animated. 'Yeah, there is,' he said, his voice rising. 'And these motherfuckers never show up when I'm being shot at.'

Steve just laughed again.

How many times have you been shot at? I asked.

'I don't even know, man! I lost count.' He pointed past us, back out into Inglewood. 'But there is bullet holes every fucking where. Look at the telephones poles, look at the motherfucking cars. Hell yeah, it's the most dangerous place to live on earth! I've seen a lot of friends got shot at, I guess I'm lucky or something, I don't know.'

He sank back against the wall as Ron approached, obviously recognising him as someone not to get too lippy in front of.

'How high were you when you did that?' asked Ron, gesturing at Darren's eyes.

'I was not high, I was sober,' he mumbled, the sudden burst of energy all gone again.

Ron was incredulous. 'You did that sober?'

'What did your mum say?' asked Steve.

'My mamma dead,' mumbled Darren. 'She ain't gonna say shit.'

'Good thing!' said Steve.

Darren looked him straight in the eye. 'Not really,' he said.

✧   ✧   ✧

Our time with Ron Lopez and the 77th Gang Unit was over. And it had not panned out like we had expected.

It hadn't been about the big busts, the major take-downs, the tense stand-offs that we'd experienced in other places – and, that one party-smashing aside, the action had all been pretty muted. But rolling with Ron had given us something different. It had been a lesson in LA's gang culture, sure – but it was also something like a lesson in how to get results in places that less dedicated cops might just write off as hopeless.

The statistics speak for themselves – bringing the murder rate down from 160 killings a year to around 35 is, like Dan Horan said, nothing short of miraculous. But the numbers don't tell the whole story. The point about the 77th Gang Unit is intelligence. Both kinds.

Ron knows these streets so well – and his understanding of all the gangs and subsets of gangs and who's friends with who and who's at war with who is what's really making the difference. Like I said: knowledge is power. And that's what's winning the war in South Central LA.

It's not just about who's toughest – it's about who's smartest.

EPILOGUE

And that was it. From the jungles of Colombia to the streets of South Central LA – and via the worst ghettoes, shanty towns, backstreets and alleyways the planet could throw at us. Every precinct we visited threw up different challenges, different problems … but they all had a couple of things in common. In these desperate, dangerous places, the only thing keeping total anarchy from taking over completely was the courage and dedication of a few good men and women.

It made me think. For most of us – back in Britain especially – the police force is something we take for granted. Being able to walk down a street without fear of getting shot or stabbed, being able to put your children to bed at night without worrying about stray bullets killing them as they sleep … these are dangers most of us don't have to deal with.

But in some parts of the world, as I saw for myself, they're a daily reality.

Becoming a cop is not a decision these guys make lightly. For a kid brought up in the colonias of El Salvador, the ghettoes of Port Moresby, the projects of Baltimore or the gang-infested streets of South Central LA, the easy option is to become a criminal – that's where the glamour, the money, the status is. Turning your back on that and choosing to uphold the law takes a whole lot more balls.

That's why I'm in awe of them. The policemen we met did it because they want to make a difference. They want to make their neighbourhoods, their cities, their countries better places. Every day they get up and go to work knowing that this one could be their last; every day they lay their own lives on the line so that ordinary citizens can have a little of the safety and security we take for granted.

It's a hell of a job. Everywhere we went around the world, we spoke to murderers, robbers, drug dealers, criminals of all kinds … and they all said the same: I wouldn't be a cop. It's just too dangerous, it's just too tough.

So are these the world's toughest cops? They're the best we could find – this time. But I can't see this being the end of the story. There has got to be more of these incredible men and women out there … and we're still looking for them.

Until next time … and like the man used to say: sleep safe. Don't have nightmares.

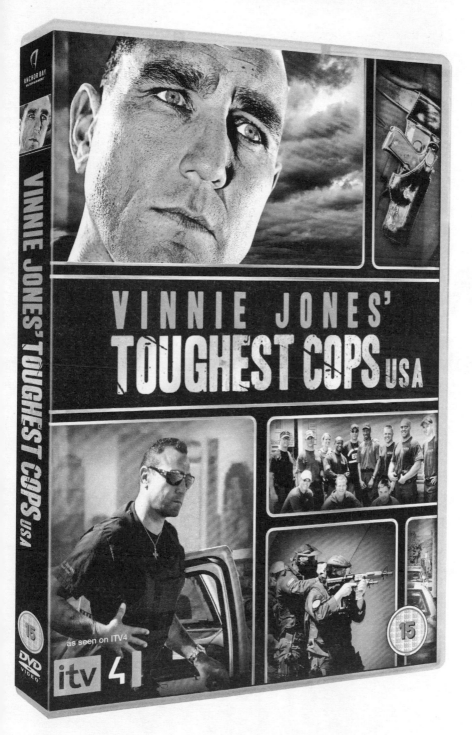